Lessons *from the* Methodist Reformation
that Will Transform Any Organization

You are the best lay leader I have ever had the pleasure of serving with. Thank you for your diligent, dedicated and excellent service. Thank you for your unwavering support. I will never forget you.

D. R. Rhodes

Lessons *from the* Methodist Reformation
that Will Transform Any Organization

Derrick R. Rhodes, Ph.D.

XULON PRESS

Xulon Press
2301 Lucien Way #415
Maitland, FL 32751
407.339.4217
www.xulonpress.com

© 2021 by Derrick R. Rhodes, Ph.D.

All rights reserved solely by the author. The author guarantees all contents are original and do not infringe upon the legal rights of any other person or work. No part of this book may be reproduced in any form without the permission of the author. The views expressed in this book are not necessarily those of the publisher.

Printed in the United States of America.

Paperback ISBN-13: 978-1-6305-0848-7
eBook ISBN-13: 978-1-6305-0849-4

TABLE OF CONTENTS

FOREWORD .... **IX**
INTRODUCTION .... **XI**

    WHAT IS THE PURPOSE OF THIS BOOK? xiii
    HOW TO USE THIS BOOK? xvi
    HOW IS THIS BOOK STRUCTURED? xvi
    Chapter 1: Change Management xvii
    Chapter 2: Change Management in the Methodist Organization ..xvii
    Chapter 3: Resistance to Change in the Methodist Organization.. xviii
    Chapter 4: Achieving Successful Organizational Change xviii
    Chapter 5: Conclusion: Where Do You Start? xix

CHAPTER 1: CHANGE MANAGEMENT 1

    LEARNING OBJECTIVES 1
    TERMS FOR UNDERSTANDING ORGANIZATIONAL CHANGE . 3
    Change 3
    Change Agents 14
    Internal Change Agents 18
    Structural Change Agents.................................... 19
    People Change Agents 20
    Organization 21
    Organizational Culture...................................... 25
    Types of Organizational Cultures 27
    Influences on Organizational Culture 31
    Organizational Change Management 33
    Planned Change Management 39
    Emergent Change Management.............................. 42

Equity Theory 46
Expectancy Theory 48
Maslow's Hierarchy of Needs 50
Organizational Commitment 51
Self-Efficacy 53
Transformational Leadership 55
Organizational Readiness for Change 57
REVIEW QUESTIONS 60

Chapter 2: Change Management in the Methodist Organization 63

LEARNING OBJECTIVES 63
THE DEBATABLE QUESTION 65
THE FORCES FOR THE STATUS QUO AND FORCES
    FOR CHANGE 71
Forces for the Status Quo 73
Forces for Change 76
External forces for change 94
REVIEW QUESTIONS 98

Chapter 3: Resistance to Change in the Methodist Organization 101

LEARNING OBJECTIVES 101
TWO FORMS OF RESISTANCE 102
REASONS FOR RESISTANCE 104
NINE LESSONS FROM RESISTANCE TO CHANGE 105
REVIEW QUESTIONS 107

Chapter 4: Achieving successful organizational change .109

LEARNING OBJECTIVES 109
ORGANIZATIONAL LESSONS LEARNED FROM THE
    METHODIST DILEMMA 110
Establish a Change Team 111
Understand How Change Plans Work 112

Learn Change Models and Choose One 116
THE METHODIST ORGANIZATIONAL CHANGE METHOD .. 123
Choose Change Agents With Courage 128
Set Goals and Priorities for the Change Team 129
Challenge the Organizational Culture, Vision, and Goals 130
Prepare for the change *131*
Deal with the fears *131*
Deal with what is and what is not 132
Choose Transformational Leadership to Articulate the Vision 133
Overcome Resistance to Change 139
Leadership Qualities to Overcome Resisters *141*
Connect the Change to the Larger Vision *143*
REVIEW QUESTIONS 147

CHAPTER 5: CONCLUSION: WHERE DO YOU START? 149

LEARNING OBJECTIVES 149
LEARN REASONS FOR CHANGE 150
LEARN REASONS PEOPLE FEAR CHANGE 151
LEARN ORGANIZATIONAL LESSONS FOR SUCCESSFUL
    ORGANIZATIONAL CHANGE 152
SHARE THE IMPACT OF ORGANIZATIONAL CHANGE 154
MATCH YOUR WORDS WITH YOUR ACTIONS 155
REVIEW QUESTIONS 160

ACKNOWLEDGMENTS 161
REFERENCES 165

FOREWORD

THE REVEREND (DR.) DERRICK R. RHODES PROVIDES A DIStinctive historical aspect of a pivotal duration in time and space of transformative leadership in the United Methodist Church and how internal, external, and blended environmental forces impacted the Church. He reconciles what happened in decision making from 1939 to 1968 by church leaders and laity that resonates in current events regarding inclusivity.

The Church operates with a universal, welcoming, inviting, and authentic wholeness as a representative institution of the Holy Trinity for team building and moving people, organizations, and institutions from good to great. Strategic usages of organization leadership, change, development, and management attributes are essential to improving people, processes, systems, structures, and organizations.

Dr. Rhodes' book, *Lessons From the Methodist Reformation That Will Transform Any Organization*, offers lessons after each chapter, instrumental in building people, teams, and organizations. He articulates how to empower teams for producing enhanced organizational structure, vitality, wins, and outcomes. Dr. Rhodes encapsulates this within Scripture (e.g., 1 Cor. 12:12-27 and Gal. 3:26-28). Each chapter's lesson objectives will drive individual and team participants to reflect, meet, filter, plan, evaluate, and celebrate contextual keys for accomplishing significant initiatives, missions, and ministries for the Body of Jesus Christ. He explains organizational change management tools, models, and theories to improve public, private, and hybrid organizations within a particular context and content for evaluating processes and increasing performance outcomes.

Dr. Rhodes engages readers, participants, and scholars in problem resolution by identifying what happened in the past to what is possible for today and in the future. Decision making from the era of the Central Jurisdiction creation and the united church efforts implicates, freezes, and frees the United Methodist Church and overall society about acceptance, racial and ethnic equities, diversity, and inclusivity issues relevant in the real world today.

Historical events, formations, and developments help shape where the Church goes from here to improve future outcomes. The book highlights how organizational change management opportunities amid problematic institutional policies, practices, and patterns that people, teams, and organizations can thrive regardless of competing forces intentional or unintentional or latent.

Reverend Joe Flowers, Jr.
Retired United Methodist Elder

INTRODUCTION

FIX IT OR DIE. DURING THE 16TH CENTURY, THE PROTESTANT Reformation was a religious, political, intellectual, and cultural turbulent flow that fractured Catholic Europe (Schilling, 1986; Tracy, 1999). This turbulence planted a seed that sprung up like rosebuds into the structures and beliefs that would characterize the region in the modern era. Northern and Central Reformers took root, such as Martin Luther, John Calvin, and Henry VIII, who defied papal authority and questioned the Catholic Church's power to delineate Christian praxis. They put up a fight for a religious and political restructuring of power that would put more authority into pastors' hands. The revolt sparked conflicts, oppressions, tortures, and the so-called Antithetical Reformation, which was ultimately the Catholic Church's brutal reaction to the Protestants.

Similar to the Protestant Reformation, there was a Methodist Reformation that started in the 19th century. This reformation was a political, intellectual, and cultural cataclysm that characterized Methodism worldwide, creating the structures and beliefs that would define the Methodist Church in years to come. With throttled ambition and infinite optimism and faith, reformers such as James Thomas (who later became a Bishop in the Church), Mary McCleod Bethune, Joseph Lowery, Robert Elijah Jones, and Charles C. Parlin challenged the Methodist Church.

These reformers also questioned the Methodists' belief to systematize African Americans in a separate jurisdiction for their own sake and the purpose of unity of the Methodist Church. From African Americans' perspectives, they did not feel like they were entirely a part of the Methodist organization. Consequently, this practice of separatism conveyed the wrong message about the Body of Christ segment called Methodists.

God calls the Body of Christ to be a team. Ecclesiastes 4:9-12 (Common English Translation) says,

> Two are better than one because they have a good return for their hard work. If either should fall, one can pick up the other. But how miserable are those who fall and don't have a companion to help them up! Also, if two lie down together, they can stay warm. But how can anyone stay warm alone? Also, one can be overpowered, but two together can put up resistance. A three-ply cord doesn't easily snap.

In Proverbs 27:17 (Common English Translation), we hear these words: "As iron sharpens iron, so one person sharpens a friend." An organization's effectiveness is due to effective teams working together as an organized body, which produces better outcomes (Maxwell, 2010). Teamwork enhances organizational success, organizational productivity, and administrative support. Effective teams are vital for organizations to stay globally competitive and productive (Reich, 1987).

Some in the Methodist organization did not see African Americans as a full part of the body. We were players, which we so desperately wanted to be, but not players on the Methodist team. In their research on groups, Cohen and Bailey (1997) revealed four types of teams: work, parallel, project, and management. These four groups possess a common purpose and appropriate skills and resources and can work through conflict (Hsiang, 2002). Members respect, trust, and care for each other.

Some in the Methodist Church viewed African Americans as not possessing any appropriate skills or assets, such as respect for each other, conflict resolution skills, and resources to help the Methodist people impact the world in a meaningful way. They felt African Americans were limited in their abilities. They also thought that these below par abilities would negatively impact the Methodist people's global evangelistic efforts. Herein lies the problem in early Methodism.

Many of these erroneous beliefs led the Methodist Church to exclude its Black members. As you read this book about the change management process in the Methodist denomination, you will discover how the Methodist organization changed its ways from exclusion to inclusion. The Methodist group used a change management process that eventually worked to make its establishment better.

WHAT IS THE PURPOSE OF THIS BOOK?

I grappled with and raised the same question that Davis (2008) posed in *The Methodist Unification: Christianity and the Politics of Race in the Jim Crow Era*: "How did these Methodists—nearly eight million strong" (p. 5) envisage what they formed in 1939 and call it a union "when members in the Church body were racially divided?" (p. 5). I struggled with what process could change such an entrenched separatist view.

With these questions in mind, the purpose of this book is to examine the implications and significance of the change management process when the Methodist organizational structure dismantled the racially structured territory called the Central Jurisdiction. One of the prime priorities in organizations all across the globe is organizational change, yet studies have shown that 70% of planned change processes fail (Kotter, 1996; Hammer & Champy, 2006). This book will extract the lessons from the Methodist Reformation that can transform any organization by exploring the following questions:

1. How did the racial dilemma emerge in Methodism?
2. How was the racial dilemma in the Methodist Church finally resolved?
3. What organizational changes were needed in the Methodist organization?
4. What structural changes were required to implement the process of change?
5. What problems were anticipated, recognized, and resolved as barriers to growth?
6. Based on the Methodist Reformation, what lessons are applicable for transforming organizations today?

The goal of this book is to discover the methods of organizational change Methodist Reformation leaders used. The goal is also to unearth what leadership style Methodist utilized during the

Introduction

various stages of negotiations. I designed this book to be a case study. Why?

The phenomenon was a real event, which allowed me to procure descriptive accounts (Yin, 2014) and empowered me to grasp, analyze, comprehend, and present the situation (Patton, 2002). It allowed me to use exploratory, descriptive, and analytical research methods to answer why and how. Why was the Central Jurisdiction created? How was it eradicated? In this book, here is some of the information you will find:

- The definition of change management
- The change that took place in the Methodist Church as a result of organizational transformation
- The forces of change in the Methodist Church
- The individuals who resisted change
- The steps to transforming any organization
- A brief history of the all-Black jurisdiction
- A brief history of the Northern and Southern Methodist Episcopal Churches
- Organizational change lessons

Reading this book will advance your understanding of how to transform any organization. It will help lead your organization to a new future. You will learn how to launch a change team, how change models work, and why you should choose change agents with courage as well as how to set goals and priorities for the change team, challenge the culture, challenge the vision, and challenge the plans. Sometimes ideas can be as vague as dreams. In this book, you will learn about the type of leadership you need to choose to help you articulate the vision, overcome resistance to change, and connect the change's spark to the broader vision.

HOW TO USE THIS BOOK?

You do not have to read *Lessons From the Methodist Reformation That Will Transform Any Organization* chapter by chapter, nor do you have to read them in any particular order. However, I recommend that you read Chapter 1, which gives you background information about the problems that sparked the Methodist Reformation (the need for organizational change). I designed this book to use the Table of Contents to immediately obtain the information you need to address your most urgent problems.

You can choose a chapter that meets your needs. For those who love history, or if you prefer to analyze and apply principles once you understand a situation's background, I recommend that you begin with Chapter 1. If you want to get started transforming your organization, I recommend that you go to Chapter 4. However, please keep in mind that there are various lessons throughout this book to help you with every step you take toward your goal.

HOW IS THIS BOOK STRUCTURED?

I divided *Lessons From the Methodist Reformation That Will Transform Any Organization* into five chapters. Following is a summary of what you will discover in each chapter.

Introduction

Chapter 1: Change Management

Chapter 1 provides an introduction to the concept of change management. It explores what change management is. It begins by defining words that will help you understand how change management works. You can read about how various scholars and practitioners define change management. This chapter also gives a brief history of change. It explains why scholars and practitioners applied the change management discipline to organizations.

You can also read about the various outcomes of change management. You see how multiple scholars and practitioners explain how change management can benefit your organization.

Chapter 2: Change Management in the Methodist Organization

Chapter 2 explains why a change was necessary for the Methodist organization. You will read about the Methodist Church's beginning values and the drift from those living values. You will discover what caused turmoil in the Methodist organization, how that turmoil impacted the organization, and how it also affected the culture in which the Methodist organization existed at the time.

You will learn how American culture impacted the Methodist organization and how the Methodist culture impacted America. You will read about how various leaders grappled with maintaining the organization as it was. You will also learn about others who were vocal about changes.

In Chapter 2, you will also get to the essence of change agents' roles and their roles in organizational change. You will learn why change agents are the backbone of the change process. I start with the multifunction of change agents. I highlight how various scholars and practitioners define the roles of change agents. You can also learn about what qualities change agents need to possess to be successful.

You can discover the two types of forces of change and the difference between them. You will learn how those two forces changed the Methodist Church's organizational structure and how they can change your organization.

Chapter 3: Resistance to Change in the Methodist Organization

Change does not happen without some resistance. There are various forms of resistance. Chapter 3 highlights some of those forms of resistance during the Methodist Church's organizational change process. I show you who they were and how they resisted. I also explore the various ways to handle opposition. Learning to cope with resistance is key to success in your organizational change process.

Chapter 4: Achieving Successful Organizational Change

In Chapter 4, I explain additional lessons learned from the change process that took place in the Methodist Church to do away with the all-Black church area. I also help you explore five models of change that your organization can implement to change its culture. From the five models, I highlight the change model that the Methodist forces for change used to eliminate the Central Jurisdiction, change the Methodist organizational structure, and change Methodist corporate culture. You will learn the specific lessons, components, and steps you need to improve your horizon experiences, organizational structure, and culture.

Chapter 5: Conclusion: Where Do You Start?

In Chapter 5, you learn where you need to start your organizational change. I will also emphasize the necessary steps for accomplishing the change you desire so that your dreams about your organization come true.

Chapter 1
Change Management

LEARNING OBJECTIVES

- Explain the history of change management.
- Define the terms needed to understand the phenomenon called change management.
- Describe what happens as a result of the change.
- Discuss what happens if the change is positive.
- Discuss what happens if the change is negative.
- Explain how an organization functions when its members define it as an organism.
- Discuss what an organization needs to thrive.
- Define culture.

- Define organizational culture.
- Explain the various types of corporate cultures.
- Summarize the influences on culture.
- Describe what organizational change management is.
- Define planned management.
- Define emergent change management.
- Contrast planned management and emergent change management.
- Explain the equity theory.
- Explain the expectancy theory.
- Explain Maslow's hierarchy of needs.
- Discuss organizational commitment.
- Discuss self-efficacy.
- Define transformational leadership.
- Explain organizational readiness.

CHANGE MANAGEMENT, AS A KNOWN PRACTICED DISCIPLINE, emerged about 40 years ago. In the 1990s, this discipline appeared on the scene. There were no professional change managers, organized disciplines, or transferable approaches besides in psychology. During the 1990s, scholars and practitioners began applying the principle of change and change procedures to organizations.

With the rise of globalization, changing cultures, and the migration of various nationalities, religions, and ethnicities, the need for understanding how to process change was vital to leaders', managers', and organizations' survival. This chapter highlights various organizational terminologies. It also draws attention to Methodist history and how organizational constituents use corporate terms in organizational change. Understanding these terms will help you and your business grasp the corporate leadership field of practice and make learning about this topic more conducive and productive.

TERMS FOR UNDERSTANDING ORGANIZATIONAL CHANGE

Change

Let us start with the term *change*. *Cambridge Dictionary* defines organizational change as "A process in which a large company or organization changes its working methods or aims, for example, to develop and deal with new situations or markets" ("Organizational Change," 2020).

The slavery issue. When the Methodist Church first came out of its womb, it took a progressive stance on racial issues. Founder John Wesley made it clear that he saw slavery as one of the evilest social systems ever invented (Thomas, 1992). It was barbaric. He saw the horrors of slavery, the middle passages, the forced voyages of shackled and enslaved Africans aboard slave ships, buying and owning people as slaves as incompatible with Christian living and faith.

Wesley was so committed to his feelings about this evil malady called slavery that he drafted a tract called *Thoughts Upon Slavery* at age 70. According to Semmel (1973), Scripture was not the idea that moved Wesley's heart about forced African bondage. Instead, his Arminian sensibility stirred him to speak against the horrors of slavery. With forceful passion, he described the capture of Africans by force or by deceit. He also expressed intensely the cruelness of the middle passage, the humiliation of selling human beings, the hard labor, and the brutal punishments administered to Africans.

Wesley uttered in no uncertain terms that slavery was wrong. It was against the natural laws. After working out his thoughts against the inhumanity of slavery and putting his thoughts in writing, Wesley then sent his tract to one of his friends. About a year later, Wesley published the pamphlet.

In this booklet, Wesley laid out his argument. He stated that slavery was a product of an immoral time and only reared its ugly head because America needed inexpensive labor to harvest its crops. Furthermore, to expound his stream of consciousness and vent his feelings to those who thought that slavery saved Africans from hunger and self-destruction, Wesley, in contrast, replied that this argument was a fallacy and based in error.

People distributed this tract throughout England and America. In that tract, Wesley made it clear what he wanted for slaves: "O burst thou all their chains in sunder: Thou Savior of all, make them free, that they may be free indeed" (Smith, 1986, p. 148). Wesley saw all people as free human beings.

The Methodist Church became well known as an antislavery Church. The burning desire to see those bonded by chains moved many clergy and laity involved in the Abolitionist Movement. To be sure, they played a vital role in ending slavery. Murray (2004), in *Methodists and the Crucible of Race, 1939-1975*, explained, "In 1780, Methodist ministers meeting in Baltimore declared slavery, 'contrary to the laws of God, man and nature and hurtful to society, contrary to the dictates of conscience and pure religion'" (p. 11). Furthermore, Murray stated, ministers in 1785, who wrote the first Methodist *Discipline,* rallied against the practice of slavery. These ministers made it mandatory that in 2 years, members had to set their slaves free.

Many harbored doubts that this rule would stand. Those feelings of distrust were not in error because a critical number of Southern Methodists who were slaveholders were so adamantly against this disciplinary action that they fought against the rule. Six months after the practice to set slaves free was ratified, it was postponed (W. W. White, 2009).

Even though the Methodist Church postponed the rule, it still required its pastors and bishops who owned slaves to maintain the polity of the Church during the practice of slavery in America (W. W. White, 2009). History clearly shows that this slavery issue kept dogging Methodists like their own shadows. It continued to stir the collective conscience of some Americans. It continued to hobble the human actions that could heal the Church. It continued to be a point of conflict. But, despite the unrelenting, lingering issue of slavery, some in the Methodist Church remained robust and unmuffled voices against it.

The live-let-live ideology. There were several attempts to coerce the Church to temper its subjugation language. Nevertheless, according to W. W. White (2009), Methodist officials could not convince the Southern Methodist to temper its slavery nomenclature. No matter how some in the Church explained that the Methodist Church was structurally weak—an institution with clay feet—as long as the racial dilemma existed, the message still fell on deaf ears.

The Methodist Church's deaf ear syndrome was manifested, Murray (2004) asserted, by the Church's actions. In 1804, the Methodist Church decided to tackle this concrete problem by putting forth a particular *live-let-live* ideology and even formulated two *Books of Disciplines*. The Southern Methodist book had no language against slavery. However, the Northern Methodist Church marched to a beat of a different drummer. It continued to declare in its *Discipline* a loud voice against holding slaves in any form or fashion.

The separation. Ultimately, this war over slavery raged so much that, in 1844, the Church separated into two different denominations: the Methodist Episcopal Church (MEC; Northern Church) and the Methodist Episcopal Church, South (MECS; Southern Church; W. W. White, 2009). Because the Methodist Church was a large and influential denomination, this separation, according to McEllhenney, Maser, Rowe, and Yigoyen (1992), impacted Methodist people and the broader society by intensifying the political disunity in the nation. The historical record shows that these two similar denominations remained separated for almost a century.

The birth of the Central Jurisdiction. After almost a century of being separated over slavery, the Methodist Church reunited in 1939. In 1844 and 1939, the Methodist Church reflected the society of that time and not the Body of Christ, a multicultural team in action together for good (Thomas, 1992), which Paul described in 1 Corinthians 12:12-27 and Galatians 3:28. In 1 Corinthians 12:12-13, Paul compared the church to a human body. He said that the body has many parts, all the pieces are necessary, and all the details have a specific function. Even though the human body's characteristics are different, they have to work together if the body is to survive and function properly. Paul said this is how the church is— many people from various backgrounds, races, and nationalities, both male and female.

Paul proclaimed this is the new tenet of our faith: although we are many, with differences, for the Church to survive and serve effectively, we have to work collectively. In Galatians 3:28, Paul emphasized that although we are different, we should not allow the differences to separate us or make one group feel better than or superior to the other team members. In 1844 and 1939, the Methodist Church missed this portion of Paul's message. Because they did, they created a great dilemma, an invisible church, a racial organizational reality, which they then struggled with for years (McClain, 1984; Thomas, 1992). The treacherous waters of race continued to pound against the walls of the Church. How was the great dilemma set in motion?

In 1916, the MEC and Methodist Church, South (MECS) established the Joint Commission on Unification (later called the Joint Commission), whose responsibility it was to develop a comprehensive plan of merger (Davis, 2008; Frank, 2006; Norwood, 1974; Thomas, 1992). The Joint Commission devised several draft proposals before developing an idea that was approved by both conferences. In 1935, Methodist formed a Plan of Union, consisting of five White jurisdictional conferences divided by region and composed of White-only gatherings. The plan also called for one jurisdictional territory to house all the Methodist Church's African American constituents.

During the Uniting Conference, the Methodist body presented the 1935 Plan of Union, and the conference approved it. Three Methodist bodies [MEC, MECS, and Methodist Protestant Church (MPC)] agreed to unite (Davis, 2008; Kirk, 2005; Norwood, 1974; Thomas, 1992). The Methodist Protestant Church separated from the Methodist Episcopal Church in November 1830. During the

Lessons from the Methodist Reformation that Will Transform Any Organization

early part of the 19th century, a reform group of clergy and laity advocated for the Methodist Organization to place more authority in clergy's and laity's hands. This reform group did not want bishops to appoint district superintendents (DS). They wanted the conference to elect DS. They also wanted the local pastors to have full membership.

And finally, they wanted to be involved more in policy-making decisions. Because the Methodist Church voted down these reformers' proposals, this group left the church and established the MPC. When the Methodist Church decided to unite in 1939, the MPC decided to be a part of the new Methodist movement. The Methodist Church was on the verge of merging three branches of Methodism.

However, the agreement stipulated that all the African American members in all three denominations—MEC, MECS, and Methodist Protestant Church—would have to be grouped into a separate jurisdiction for the plan to be consummated. Based on this agreement, the Methodist Church placed 19 African American annual conferences in a jurisdiction named the Central Jurisdiction, which was the sole jurisdiction created based on race and not geography.

When the Methodist had the opportunity to reimage itself as a racially inclusive Church, a more enduring canopy, it instead chose the exclusivity road. This approach was almost like a slap in the face, indicating that the Church—smug, detached, and dogmatic—refused to hear the pains of its African American members. For African Americans, the 1939 plan made a disastrous debut. It was an unimaginable nightmare.

Blatantly, Dr. James Thomas (1992) spoke that it sounded like a paradox. For the Caucasian Methodists, the conference's uniting was a glorious day, an emotional crescendo with nods of agreement.

For the African American Methodists who waited with bated breath, it was a day filled with hurt, frustration, and resentment.

According to Dr. Thomas (1992), the 47 African American delegates who attended the 1939 Uniting Conference carried no illusions about what was happening to them; they were racially compartmentalized and marginalized. Therefore, 36 voted against the Plan of Union, and 11 abstained.

James P. Brawley (1967), the president of Clark College (later Clark-Atlanta University), in Atlanta, Georgia, delineated with clarity, power, and insight the hopes and feelings of African American Methodist members on that disappointing day:

> It was the hope of the Negro membership of the Methodist Episcopal Church that his status would be improved in the new United Church and that no structural organization would set him apart and give him less dignity and recognition than he already had . . . He therefore rejected the Plan of Union . . . This was a stigma too humiliating to accept. (p. 3)

Gilbert Caldwell (2012), a civil rights activist and retired United Methodist minister, expressed that his father, who was a preacher, attended the unification conference. Caldwell's father shared how hurt and wounded he and other African American delegates were when Methodists formed the all-African American conference. McClain (1984) explained it was a compromise that abused, insulted, and disappointed African American Methodists. The Unification spoke loudly that the Methodist Church did not want to be one church. According to Dr. W. Astor Kirk (2005), in his book *Desegregation of the Methodist Church Polity*, unification was a decision to protect the great dilemma's constitutionality.

As a swarm of Caucasian Methodist Church members sang "We Are Marching to Zion" after Methodists adopted the Plan of Union, the African American delegates remained in their seats with senses stunned and weeping (Brawley, 1967; McClain, 1984). The fraternal order that many African Americans had hoped for was defeated. Their hopes became like bubbles blown up in the air. It was a step backward, not a step forward to racial equality and full representation in the Church that so many African Americans loved.

Again, the Church that Methodism launched in 1744 in Baltimore, Maryland, became—on April 26, 1939, in Kansas City, Missouri—two separate organizations. What looked like unity was not unity.

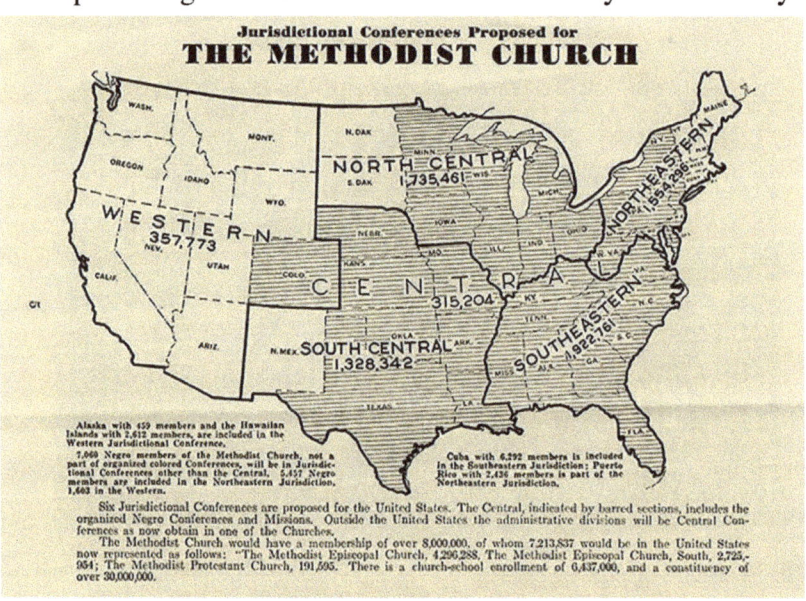

The map highlights the proposed jurisdictional conferences for the 1939 merger creating the Methodist Church. Five of the jurisdictions are based on geography, while the shaded area representing the Central Jurisdiction would segregate African American Methodists from the rest of the denominational structure. Map courtesy of Pitts Theology Library, Emory University.

This separation between African Americans and Whites was nothing new because they were separate in previous structures (Davis, 2008; Thomas, 1992) and because, as Thomas Frank (2006) articulated so well, "church polity is sometimes worked out on the backs of the voiceless" (p. 92). By implementing this new structure, the Church was adding another racial layer between the races. McClain (1984) called it a church-within-a-church. It was a Jim Crow system within the Methodist denomination.

The Jim Crow system, enacted in the late 19th and early 20th centuries, were state and local laws that required racial segregation in the Southern States of the United States of America. This same type of Jim Crow structure was introduced, adapted, and advanced in Methodism. This diabolical system impeded the Body of Christ's progress because it would not allow African Americans to be fully activated in the redemptive work of Jesus Christ in the Methodist Church.

When Supreme Court Chief Justice Earl Warren (1954) wrote his opinion in the *Brown v. the Board of Education* case, he penned,

> Segregation of white and colored children in public schools has a detrimental effect upon the colored children. The impact is greater when it has the sanction of the law; for the policy of separating the races is usually interpreted as denoting the inferiority of the Negro group. A sense of inferiority affects the motivation of a child to learn. Segregation with the sanction of the law, therefore, has a tendency to [retard] the educational and mental development of Negro children and to deprive

them of some of the benefits they would receive in a racial[ly] integrated school system. (para. 24)

Although Chief Justice Warren's opinion arrived long after the 1939 Plan of Union, Blacks in the Central Jurisdiction would have seen this ruling not only applying to Black children but also Black adults. African Americans whose arms and legs were being shackled by this new Body called the Central Jurisdiction saw their religious, spiritual, and educational development hampered. They saw the Black jurisdiction as a giant standing in the valley with a javelin, a spear, and a sword in its hands, depriving them of the benefits they would receive from entering an inclusive Community of Christ.

The Methodist organization produced a Body of Christ within a Body of Christ, a system that diminished African Americans' status and role in the House of God. Like the possessing of slaves, this new structure was a mistake, and it needed to be changed.

The organization change lesson: The lesson here is this: several scholars have interpreted change as a factor that your organization will have to move through successfully to maintain your company's brand within your industry (Barnett & Carroll, 1995; Cochran, Bromley, & Swando, 2002). This growth entails progressing from the familiar to the unfamiliar. This unfamiliar territory that your organization journeys toward will create uncertainties that could impede your business's organizational confidence, abilities, and performance. Consequently, a typical response to changes you want and need to make will be for some of your members to go counter to the changes by resisting them.

As your organizational turnaround from a low-performing organization takes shape, evolution emerges, which leads to transformation (Rahschulte, 2007). If the response to your organizational changes is positive, then commitment and performance will bloom. However, if the answer is negative, the reverse is true—your organization member's responsibility and performance will wither on the vine. As you go where your organization may not have gone before, be mindful that change is not easy.

Resistance to change can be almost as untamable as flies. Burke and Litwin (1992) wrote that the endless variables, the situation, the internal and external cultures, and human resistance join forces making change "difficult to predict and almost impossible to control" (p. 273). Leaders who transform their organizations hope to achieve better performance, increased profits, and improved markets (Desplaces, 2005). However, the opposite could result from negative emotions, too much change at once, and nonsupport from organizational members. If your business does not handle the transition properly, then change can shatter your organization.

Change will not be easy because your organization's leaders may not see failure in the cards. Nevertheless, you need to be honest with your organizational members that failing once or twice (or even more) is an option. Unless your leaders see it this way, they will eventually strangle the life out of your establishment's chances for success. Missing the mark is a part of the change process. As you seek to change, no matter how gently you walk, you will make mistakes.

Failing uncovers what does not work, what needs to be adjusted more, and what skills need to be enriched and upgraded the next time as the change moves forward. If you're not failing now and then, it's a signal you're not doing anything groundbreaking, out-of-the-box, or cutting-edge. Change processes that are worth their salt all factor in failure as steps toward a brighter future. The Methodist Church leadership made several misguided and botched attempts to change the Methodist structure. Like the Methodists learned, as you seek to transform yourself, you need to be aware you will probably fail more than once.

Change Agents

Your agents of change will be people who foster and empower your organization to change. They will encourage new ways to operate. In essence, they will be the type of people who will drive into your organization like a tank in fast forward and hit your business with their talents to refocus your organization's flight path.

After the Methodist Church created the Central Jurisdiction, African Americans made a vow to move heaven and earth to pull the plug on the jurisdiction that had been invented just for them. The Bishops of the all-African American area declared they would not give up; they would work until the day the Methodist Church found a more excellent way. In 1960, the Methodists' legislative body elected the Commission of Seventy to investigate the racial structure and make recommendations to remove it.

After the Commission of Seventy had studied the Church's race problem and advocated no change to the racial system, Dr. Kirk, from the New Orleans area and a layperson and staff member of the General Board of Christian Social Concerns, had a revelation about forming a committee. This committee would consist of several people chosen from within the Central territory who would challenge the Church corpus juris of forced segregation. Challenging an unjust system was nothing new to Dr. Kirk. He was a known social activist. He earned his Ph.D. from the University of Texas graduate school, which he helped to desegregate.

Dr. Kirk (Kirk, 2005) shared his idea with Dr. Brawley about forming a group that would take a stand against the Church's coerced separatism law. After listening to his point of view, Dr. Brawley told Dr. Kirk to convey the concept to the Committee. Dr. Kirk then wrote a resolution outlining his idea, which was adopted.

The Church would handpick the Committee to work shoulder to shoulder to show segregation to the door. In addition, they would provide active moral leadership and devise progressive policies for the Methodist organization. They had a gargantuan job. This new committee's quest was to do what Abraham Lincoln sought to do in the Union: help people of all races find "mutual respect, the sense of common duties and common interest which arise when men take the trouble to understand one another and to associate for a common object" (Goodwin, 2018, p. 344). The Church formed this group to help craft a life for African Americans in an inclusive form of Methodism.

After much exchange of views and bones of contention, pastor and civil rights leader Dr. Joseph E. Lowery proposed establishing the specific members chosen to serve on the study committee. Dr. Lowery recommended that

> The five-member committee should be one from each area, without regard to orders, appointed by the College of Bishops, to work in conjunction with the Jurisdictional Committee on Christian Social Concerns

and the representatives on the Commission on Interjurisdictional Relations, and to study the broader aspects of problems and adjustments. ("Journal of the Sixth Session," n.d., p. 118)

The College of Bishops appointed people who understood the Church's organization and the global effect of the continued practice of racial segregation. The five members were Dr. James Thomas who chaired the Committee; Dr. John H. Graham from the Nashville area and a staff member of the General Board of Mission; Reverend John J. Hicks from the St. Louis area and pastor of Union Memorial Church; Attorney Richard C. Erwin from the Baltimore area; and Dr. W. Astor Kirk. These five men were considered change agents.

In 1963, *The New York Times* defined the phrase *change agent* as "a result orientated individual able to accurately and quickly resolve complex tangible and intangible problems. Energy and ambition [are] necessary for success" ("Display advertisement #105," 1963, p. 26). Change agents have multiple roles that define the problem, devise the solution, and implement the plan. Change agents' tasks include providing feedback, linking others to resources, mediating differences, and managing the process (Winstead, 1982). Evans (1982) described change agents as innovators or creative mavericks who take the road less traveled.

Researchers have not researched, as much, the best change agents for various situations; however, some research has focused on the multiple types of change agents. Nikolaou, Gouras, Vakola, and Bourantas (2007) indicated that your business must choose the right kind of change agents for the situation for your organizational change to be successful. These people will garner support for your company's change procedures (Jick & Peiperl, 1998).

Change agents will be people in your organization whose interwoven strands of gifts and skills will aid, promote, and simplify the change process (Beckhard, 1969). They will encourage and galvanize your organization's members and teams to be responsible for any decisions made (Lawler, 1986). To transform your inefficient organization into a resourceful one, whoever is involved in the process, your change agents will advise and work in conjunction with them. (Sadler, 2001). Thus, one of your organization's goals is choosing the right change agents.

Nikolaou *et al*. (2007) wrote that the ultimate paradigm for change in your establishment is for every member in your organization to be empowered to be change agents. Every corporate member in your company can be a change agent if given the right situation and possess the required skills to some degree. However, this is not always possible; this is why your organization needs to be familiar with the types of change agents so that your business can make the appropriate and wise choices to aid with your corporation's organizational metamorphosis.

It is also essential for your business, church, school, or government to be familiar with change agents' types because embracing the right change agents will help better engineer ways to get people to buy into the change. Additionally, choosing the right change agent will help you better design a shared vision and educate organizational members about the change's value. The Black conference carefully chose the Committee of Five. These five were internal agents, structural change agents, and people agents. The Church gave them the task "to plan a denomination civil rights strategy and to lead a broad-scale coordinated and sustained assault on the bastions of involuntary 'racial' segregation in The Methodist Church" (Kirk, 2005, p. 63).

Internal Change Agents

Your internal change agents will be people inside your organization who will directly or indirectly impact change. Because members of the Central Jurisdiction felt the Commission on Interjurisdictional Relations would not truly work to find a more excellent way for the Methodist system to include African Americans in the Church in toto, the Central Region established an internal committee (The Committee of Five) that would.

Internal change agents work to transform organizations from within. Sometimes they are members of the organization; sometimes they are not (Beckhard, 1969; Cawsey, Deszca, & Ingols, 2012). They seek to induce change through various pressuring strategies, such as mass demonstrations, boycotts, civil disobedience, and sometimes violence. Change agents who are part of the organization are extremely useful in making changes because they understand the organizational structure (Saka, 2002).

Your internal change agents' understanding of the structure means that they know information about the organization that someone from the outside would not (Cawsey et al., 2012). It also means your inside agents would have personal leadership and organizational information that would not be accessible to external actors. They would understand employees, where to start with change, and where to implement change policies and decisions immediately. Also, the inside agents are invested in the organization because whatever happens will personally impact them. The people chosen to serve on the Committee of Five, especially Dr. Brawley, who had served on the Commission on Interjurisdictional Relations, understood the thinking and strategies of those who opposed eliminating the Central Jurisdiction.

Structural Change Agents

To achieve an organization's objectives, organizations establish a pattern of interaction among their various organizational divisions. The structure is the procedure of responsibilities employed for the work to be accomplished. Moreover, the network is the design of business aptitude, leadership, ability, purposeful links, and arrangement.

Structural change agents involve themselves with changing the organization's design for operating. Tran and Tian (2013) argued that organizations could sometimes not meet prerequisites to procure productivity and adaptability in the organizational structure's fixed landscape. They also maintain that a change in the culture of the organization requires a change in operating procedures. Strategic considerations may make it necessary to find more integrated methods of working. For example, sometimes, it's the size or the environment or technology that makes it essential to integrate work processes. The result of changing the structure will cause the organization to operate with more efficiency.

During the 1956 General Conference session, the desegregation movement that was taking place across America put enormous pressure on the Methodist Church. One of the results was that the Methodist Church proposed adding an Amendment, called

Amendment IX, to its Constitution. Amendment IX laid down the process for transferring a local church and an entire Central Jurisdiction Conference. For example, when a local church decided it wanted to move, Amendment IX stated it could do so if it moved into the white jurisdiction where it was geographically located (Kirk, 2005). This Amendment only dealt with structural change. Changing your organization's structure does not mean it will change your organization's culture or attitudes.

To change your organization's way of life or point of view, you will have to change the way your organizational members think. If you want your establishment to be more rewarding to your people and others and profitable, you will have to change your partners' corporate mindset. You accomplish this endeavor by presenting your case that your organization needs to change. Throughout your organization's life span, your company must consistently ask the questions:

- Are we routinely achieving our goals?
- Are we better today than we were yesterday? If we are not, then why?
- What are some steps we can take that will be significant game changers for us?

People Change Agents

People change agents give their attention mainly to helping individuals evolve. They focus on changing individual organizational members' attitudes, absenteeism, efficiency, and morale. They see a link "between human behavior in organizational settings, the individual, organizational interface, the organization, and the environment surrounding the organizations" (Moorhead, 2010, p. 3).

The object of the change agent is to change people's behavior. People change agents postulate that if they can stimulate people to exhibit better behavior, the result will be that the organization will be transformed. P. Drucker (1954) indicated the main problem hindering organizational growth is organizational members' failure to change their approaches and behavior as fast as their organizations need them to.

The type of change agents you choose to transform your organization may be a group of only internal agents, or only structural agents, or only people agents, or maybe a group of people who are a conglomerate of the three. The type of change agent chosen to transform the Methodist organization was a combination of the three types of agents mentioned in this book. Why? There was a need for the agents to be familiar with Methodism's particular nuts and bolts.

There was also a need for agents to be knowledgeable about the Methodist organizational flowchart. And there was a need for the change agents to possess skills that would help change Methodist members' attitudes. The types of agents you need to help better your organizations will be left to your leadership team to decide. However, being familiar now with the role of internal, structural, and people agents should make that decision a little easier.

Organization

The Methodist Church before 1968 was an organization that people could have described as a psychic prison. The goal was to make it more like an organism than a prison. Before the transition of Methodism in 1968, the American culture afflicted the Methodist Church's Caucasian leadership's thinking and good sense. For example, one of the news outlets quoted one of the leaders of the MECS as saying,

> The South and our grand division of the Methodist Church believe: That the color line must be drawn firmly and unflinchingly, in State, Church, and Society, without any deviation whatsoever: and no matter what the virtues, abilities, or accomplishments of individuals may be, there must be absolute separation of social relations. (Kirk, 2005, p. 10)

This kind of thinking is one of the reasons it took so long to change the Church.

In *Image of Organizations,* Morgan (2006) gave eight metaphors to describe and define organizations: machines, brains, cultural systems, political systems, psychic prisons, instruments of domination, flux and transformation, and organisms. An organization is defined and described as a **machine** when it has a sequence of linked components organized in a coherent structure to achieve a repeatable result. When people describe an organization as a **brain**, they see the organization designed to develop data and mature. When people characterize an organization as a **cultural system,** they perceive the organization as a mini-society with its customs and classes identified by their conduct, ethics, attitudes, and practices.

When people categorize an organization as a **political system**, they view it as an institution where people wheel and deal to advance, expand their influence, and expand their specific interests. When people identify an organization as a **psychic prison**, they portray the organization as a business whose members are trapped in an approach to thinking, which restricts their creativity, ideas, and actions. When people recognize an organization as an **instrument of domination**, they sense the organizational individuals or groups force their will on others or threaten others to exploit people for personal gains. When people observe an organization as a **flux and transformation institution**, people see the business as an ebb-and-flow institution because of the environment the industry has to survive in.

Bertalanffy (1968) advocated that organizations are merely a reflection of the human body. Bertalanffy's rationale was this: both reflect multifaceted, dynamic ecosystems that continuously change. Therefore, organizations are living organisms. They are organisms that need the support of their environment to sustain their life.

When people define organizations as **organisms**, they see them as industries that must have the proper environment to live in, adapt and overcome instability, and be productive. Without a conducive environment, organizations will pass away and have a funeral and a committal service. Carney (1999) supported this idea: "Organizations ... are governed by the same laws of change that govern living things" (p. viii). The similarity that organizations have with living things means that organizations are viewed as alive, breathing creatures that evolve. They are creatures that can adapt to the ethos and move with the shifting currents, winds, and fluxes.

The similarity that organizations have with living things also means an organization can be healthy or unhealthy. In a healthy organization, the organization's limbs are appropriately aligned and move smoothly and efficiently to achieve the desired outcomes. In a healthy organization, the organization is also vibrant and proficient in its performance. All over the organization's body, there are signs it is blooming with health.

On the other hand, an unhealthy organization is diseased and sick in that its limbs are not adequately aligned to work smoothly together to reach the desired outcomes. Stress is no benefit to its immune system. There are no hope and leadership antibodies to work for it when a virus is in the vicinity. An unhealthy organization's sickness can last a short time or be perpetual.

Self-destructive behavior can also be a part of a sick organization's personality. Unhealthy organization members are low in motivation, bored, and unhappy in morale. Since some scholars and practitioners see these anemic organizations as alive, just like infections in the human body, these enterprises can be infested with a virus as tough as cast iron seeking to resist any treatment that will heal the organization.

Seeing an organization as an organism also means that change does not occur in an empty space. Instead, growth occurs inside the environment of a mutually dependent system in which change is one factor moving among other factors in the system that impact the total system environment. For instance, advancements in technology, global environment, transportation, and leadership style can help organizations change. Therefore, leaders can describe organizational change as a "transformation of an interdependent living system" (Carney, 1999, p. 4). For a majority of Caucasians, it looked like White Methodists were in what Morgan called a psychic prison. The Central Jurisdiction leaders and others were attempting to move the Church away from this psychic prison organizational arrangement to an organizational structure that was more organistic, an organization that would be more tenderhearted to the unfolding of events.

As you plan your organizational change process, it is a good idea for you to analyze what type of business you have now based on Morgan's (2006) administrative definitions. It is also a good idea to know what kind of organization you want to become. In light of Morgan's images, how you see your establishment will be a strong indicator of how you will need to attack some of your company's issues.

It will also indicate the things your organization will need to remove, keep, and strive toward to become the kind of company you want to be. For example, if you see your organization like a well-oiled machine, it is highly likely your business is rigid. It is bureaucratic. All organizations are bureaucratic in some way, but some are more than others. If you discover that your organization is too rigid and your chain of command is like a ball and chain around people's necks, your business can have great difficulty adapting to change.

Organizational Culture

We can define culture as a group of people's amassed deposit of information, order of seniority, roles, experiences, morals, viewpoints, attitudes, and meanings. It gives people their identity by embedding them with spiritual, intellectual, and emotional peculiarities. It is, in its broadest sense, a community of people's learned behaviors passed on from one generation to the next. Therefore, the organization's early leaders or founders set the culture's foundation (Kotter & Heskett, 1992).

Bishop James O. Andrews, born in Georgia and a former member of the South Carolina conference, married a woman who inherited slaves from her late husband. The Methodist leaders brought to the floor of the General Conference this issue about Bishop Andrews owning slaves. The Northerners were upset that a general superintendent possessed enslaved people. Bishop Andrew was going to resign, but he was convinced not to do so. As a result, after a 6-week session, Bishop Andrews was asked to leave. The Methodist Church's request for Bishop Andrews to resign upset the Southern delegates, which led to the Methodists splitting in 1844 into the Methodist North and the Methodist South over slavery. The church stayed this way for nearly 100 years. Slavery was a part of American culture.

From its inception, within the Methodist culture, the Church debated the problem of slavery in America. Some suggested that Methodists who owned slaves should set them free. The General Conference struggled with how to handle the issue. First, they mandated that elders set their slaves free. Then they suspended the mandate in states where the legislature said slavery was the law. Out of frustration, in 1808, the General Conference permitted each annual conference to establish its directives on how to handle the slavery matter. The American society was very much driving the Methodist organizational culture. And some say the Methodist Church was steering or sustaining the American ethos.

Culture is an interplay between people and culture, and culture and people, which means that they create each other. Culture shapes the way people learn, interact, and respond to various situations. Conversely, people's change can influence culture to change by becoming more accepting, more dissenting, or more creative.

When we combine organization and culture, we get the term *organizational culture*, which defines how your organizational members will act within your business. Whatever type of business you have, your cultural definition can be different from another company. Nevertheless, the basic description of organizational culture sets the context for an organization's entire *modus operandi*.

The description lays out the organization's shared expectations, norms, and practices, which regulate how members behave with one another. The way your organizational members should think, feel, and believe about your business, stakeholders, leaders, and followers will be influenced by your establishment's culture. Your company's customs will play a vital role in shaping your organizational behavior. In sum, your culture will drive your company's personality.

Types of Organizational Cultures

The type of organizational culture that materializes will depend on corporate members' behaviors toward their organizational values. There are strong, healthy cultures. Healthy cultures are where the members understand the organizational goals, regulations, and philosophy, and they are empowered to take the proper action when necessary.

However, there are also weak and unhealthy organizations whose lungs are sending up smoke signals of distress. Their members are unfamiliar with the beliefs, norms, traditions, and behaviors of the organization. When members of your organization do not know your organization's beliefs and values or drift away from your organization's practices and attitudes, there can be a negative effect on its culture.

There are also flat organizational cultures. These types of management styles have corporate codes of practice that do not change. They have a low degree of self-awareness. In *The Leader on the Couch*, Manfred Kets de Vries (2006) noted that throughout the world, we can find people who are incapable of identifying persistently continual patterns of behavior that have grown into a disturbed and neurotic way of life. They are in a rut. They are bent out of shape like a knotted snake and unaware of it. Flat organizations are similar in as much as they tend to remain the same. If the companies are unhealthy at the beginning, they stay that way throughout the companies' existence.

During the Unification, the great compromise of 1939, the Methodist Church lost sight of its founder John Wesley's beliefs and values. On the day of Unification, Methodist members who voted to institutionalize racism forgot about its hero, John Wesley, and his plans for the Church:

> Do all the good you can,
> By all the means you can,
> In all the ways you can,
> In all the places you can,
> At all the times you can,

> To all the people you can,
> As long as ever you can.

In 1939, they also forgot Wesley's three simple rules: "(1) Do No Harm; (2) Do Good; and (3) Stay in Love with God" (United Methodist Church, 2016, p. 78).

Wesley was adamantly against any practice that excluded any group of people from fully participating in the Church and in community life. Any system that exploited people and forced them to work as indentured servants was detrimentally opposed to Wesley's ideals. Days before his death, Wesley (1958) wrote to William Wilberforce, a British politician and a leader in the anti-slavery movement:

> Dear Sir, Unless the divine power has raised you up to be as Athanasius contra mundum, I see not how you can go through your glorious enterprise in opposing that execrable villainy, which is the scandal of religion, of England, and of human nature. Unless God has raised you up for this very thing, you will be worn out by the opposition of men and devils. But if God be for you, who can be against you? Are all of them together stronger than God? O be not weary of well-doing! Go on, in the name of God and in the power of His might, till even American slavery (the vilest that ever saw the sun) shall vanish away before it.

> Reading this morning a tract wrote by a poor African, I was particularly struck by that circumstance that a man who has black skin, being wronged or outraged by a white man, can have no redress; it being a "law" in our colonies that the oath of a black against a white goes for nothing. What villainy is this?
>
> That he who has guided you from youth up may continue to strengthen you in this and all things, is the prayer of, dear sir,
>
> Your affectionate servant,
> John Wesley (p. 153)

John Wesley believed that God created all people equally. Wesley (1958) declared, "The African is in no respects inferior to the European" (p. 280). Wesley also believed that God came to redeem the souls of every human being on the earth.

One of the main reasons for the unhealthy position the Methodist Church found itself in throughout its history was that Methodist people drifted away from its founder's core values. This floating away from these core values impacted Methodism's organizational fitness. It created a hostile culture. Intentionally, it excluded African Americans from full participation in the Church. It generated unfair practices and low morale in its African American constituents. If seeking to be healthy or seeking to move from unhealthy to healthy, your organization will need to include in your core values creating a positive culture for all your members. Your ethics will also need to involve building a culture of inclusive leadership, vibrant workplaces, and inspired members (Lowe, 2012).

Influences on Organizational Culture

Internal influences on organizational culture. One internal influence on corporate culture is people. People who enter your business come with personalities, and those traits can impact your business. Those you hire or choose to conduct your company's business can affect your bottom line and decision-making process. Their emotions can determine whether they will be good or bad workers. Also, their feelings can impact how your customers feel about your company's service. Leaders also influence your business culture. For example, if your leaders do not care about your customers' well-being, this could affect how your employees handle your clients. Internal forces can help or hinder your company's prosperity.

Methodists stitched into Methodism's constitutional fabric the forced segregated structure. Dr. Kirk felt the Methodist organization's internal influences could positively impact changing the segregated system. But the Methodist people's behavior did not convince Dr. Thomas that the Church's internal leadership would be enough to inspire change.

External influences on organizational culture. Various external influencers can impact corporate cultures, such as the economy, politicians, or competition. When there is a downturn in the economy, people become more cautious about spending their money and time. Less money for your business means less hiring and products you can offer. Politicians can have an impact on your business, as well. Their voices can help or hurt your organization. Although Dr. Kirk had confidence—it would take internal forces to undo the Central Jurisdiction—Dr. Thomas believed it would take more than internal influences to sway the Methodist Church's value system at that time; it would take external clout as well. Thomas explained to produce a change in the Methodist Church, the all-Black area of the Church would have "to look upon the social institutions in the wider society as the norms for church life" (Kirk, 2005, p. 44). He believed the fight for justice in the secular society could spill over into the Church by soliciting community help.

Influence of values on organizational culture. Values establish the organization's tone. We live in a world where performance, attitudes, and behaviors guide us. Dickson, Aditya, and Chhokar (2000) explained that the organizational culture's foundation derives from (a) the founders' values and beliefs, (b) the organization's characteristics, and (c) the society in which the organization walks the earth.

Roy Disney (n.d.), a cofounder of The Walt Disney Company, proposed that "it's not hard to make decisions when you know what your values are" (section 1). Mahatma Gandhi (n.d.) said,

> Keep your thoughts positive because your thoughts become your words. Keep your words positive because your words become your behavior. Keep your behavior positive because your behavior becomes your habits. Keep your habits positive because your habits become your values. Keep your values positive because your values become your destiny. (para. 1)

Dr. Thomas thought the Central Jurisdiction's members would have to look beyond internal help to move the Methodist Church in a new direction. He sensed that the Methodist Church's values were not yet mature enough to shape a new Methodist culture, a culture that "actively worked to eliminate discrimination on the basis of race, color or national origin" (Kirk 2005, p. 43).

The values you set for your organizations are essential. They reflect the priorities for your business. They will guide the decisions you make. Making the right decisions is more comfortable when your leaders know what is vital to your organization. Creating exact values will not hinder, hamper, or frustrate your business; it will empower your organization. So, decide your core values by having brainstorming sessions and making a list of those values.

Those values need to be operational. In other words, values are no good if your business cannot convert them into actions. You may end up with several norms that are similar. Combine those values and make one. Then make sure that your organization's vision, goals, and practices reflect those values. Exact core values that represent your company will shape your organization's destiny.

Organizational Change Management

Organizational change, organizational improvement, and organizational development have been used interchangeably (Neuman, Edwards, & Raju, 1994). An initial meaning of organizational development labeled it as utilizing behavioral science knowledge in a deliberate change effort. It is supervised from the top to improve an organization's effectiveness and health by devising interventions to aid its procedures. Changing an organization's strategies and culture is organizational management.

The goal of representatives of the Central Jurisdiction (the Committee of Five) was to design a systematic approach that would achieve Christian fellowship at all church levels. For the Central Area to achieve this organizational development, they asked Dr. Kirk (2005) to research the following:

- To analyze the potential of Amendment IX as a vehicle for desirably eliminating the Central Jurisdiction organization.
- To examine the First Report of Recommendations of the Commission on Interjurisdictional Relations. (In April 1961, the Commission issued a First Report, which included several recommendations regarding transferring annual conference organizations of the Central Jurisdiction Organization into four of the five geographical jurisdiction organizations.)
- To develop an organizational profile of the Central Jurisdiction, both as an ecclesiastical body and a corporate entity. (p. 70)

According to Kirk (2005), Amendment IX had several problems: (a) there was no process for transferring Central Jurisdiction pastors to annual conferences of a particular geographical jurisdiction; (b) a church from the African American jurisdiction might be acceptable to a geographical jurisdiction, but the pastor may be unacceptable; and (c) it was not an instrument that would improve the Methodist Church's effectiveness and health by ridding the Church of every form of racism. The Amendment IX proposal brought to the surface that there were differences between the Methodist Church and the all-Black conference regarding what the step-by-step process should ultimately accomplish.

The Methodist Church's attitude was to find a way to transfer the Central Jurisdiction's conferences to the broader Methodist Structure. It did not want to address the racial injustice of the Methodist Church's polity of separate but equal. On the other hand, the Central Territory's mindset was to devise a transfer process that smoothly transferred the Central Jurisdiction's churches to the larger Church and develop proposals and interventions to wipe out all forms of racism and exclusion in the Church. The African American jurisdictional members believed that their process and recommendations would make the Church better. It would also rid the Church of its racial cloak and present the Body of Christ's right image.

In organizational development, organizations analyze their situation to plot a course of improvement. Recardo (1995) wrote change management is the *process* an organization uses to "identify new demands or constraints that the external environment places on them, identify the strategic and operational initiatives needed to maximize organizational performance, design, implement, and evaluate appropriate initiatives" (p. 5).

Your change management process should consist of systematic approaches that help enhance your organization's performance. According to Neuman et al. (1994), the organizational change should denote specific interventions that your organization will use to advance and develop your organization.

Welbourne (2014), in her article, *"Change Management Needs Change,"* explained that change management roots are in grief studies. Change is like grieving. Change can sometimes mean losing something personal and dear to people, and loss, in most cases, is accompanied by distress. Grief and loss are synonymous. Heifetz and Linsky (2004) called attention to this: "people don't resist change, they resist loss" (p. 34). Even when change is for the better, it involves letting go of certain things, such as our everyday patterns, daily relationships, and familiar places (Seley, 2017, para. 2). Researchers observed a correlation between grieving from health-related problems and grieving among employees because of job loss and division within the organization. From this correlation, the change management theory emerges.

One change model based on Elizabeth Kubler-Ross's grieving process is called the change curve. This model has been used throughout the years to understand how people react to significant change.

Kubler-Ross and Kessler (2014) suggested that terminally ill people move through five grief stages when doctors inform them that they are terminally ill. These five stages are denial, anger, bargaining, depression, and acceptance. Later, Kubler-Ross and Kessler suggested that people could employ this same five-stage grief model to any life-changing event.

In the 1980s, around the world, scholars, practitioners, leaders, and organizations decided to apply the change curve model to change management. As a result, they discovered that organizations implement the change curve's emotional stages to predict how a declaration that things will be changing could impact various organizations' employees. I discuss the change curve model further in Chapter 5.

In essence, your change management process will involve examining your organization to see what needs to remain as is, what needs to be changed, and how to implement the changes. In other words, some things in your organization must stay, and some must die if your organization is going to make progress.

For organizations, change is an ongoing process. Flexibility is a must if organizations are to endure and be productive. The reason for change will, in the end, involve the organization determining its readiness for change where senior management must determine organizational members' willingness to change the organization's story.

There are various change rates: intermittent change, gradual change, uncomfortable progressive change, constant change, and constant painful change (S. C. Miller, 2015). There are ways that change develops: emerged, planned, contingency, and choice. There are different characteristics of change: revamping, gradual adjustment, modular transformation, and community transformation. Change management utilizes various disciplines, from behavioral and social science to anthropology and information technology. The organization's use of these disciplines is similar.

Kotter (1996) wrote that change in organizations is always the same. Sometimes this change is called total quality management, quality control, restructuring, turnaround, or cultural change. The name is different, but the meaning is the same. Kotter conducted decades of organizational change research, from large organizations like Ford to small organizations like Landmark Corporation and from organizations on the verge of closing to organizations booming in business. Kotter's research has shown that the bottom line for changing any organization is always making necessary changes to manage, cope with, and survive new, more dynamic environments. This growth process involves various methods.

Hiatt and Creasey (2012) argued that organizations usually see change management as several steps that organizations take to improve processes. These procedures are learned from repeated and various attempts to solve multiple problems and from researchers in management. These researchers have created paradigms that present organizations with step-by-step methods to change themselves.

The management experts who develop these step-by-step processes have presented these systems in articles and books and used them with clients. However, these processes many times have fallen short in that they are unclear. These methods tell *how,* but not *why.* The step-by-step transformation process of removing the Black section showed how to implement change and why it was necessary. The Committee of Five and the Central Jurisdiction Study Committee worked daily toward how and why.

Although the Methodist organization constituted various committees, the Committee of Five and the Central Jurisdiction Study helped synthesize the myriad of processes and reasons to disassemble the all-Black jurisdiction. The committees helped the Black Church to move toward speaking with one voice.

As your organization travels forward in your change process, it needs to do the following: (a) tell how the change will happen but never forget to emphasize repeatedly the reasons for the change; (b) grasp that change is universal, ongoing, and varied; (c) understand that change affects everyone in your organization in some way and, therefore, everyone in the organization needs to be included in the change process; and (d) work always day and night to get everyone on the same page as much as possible.

Planned Change Management

For decades, two leading methods—planned and emergent—branded organizational change management. Organizations employ a blend of both ways in some places throughout change management. Van der Voet, Groeneveld, and Kuipers (2014) contended that the development of both methods frequently involves undertakings that help to augment and explain the change objectives for people to comprehend better and individually partake in the change process. Both methods' development means that organizations judiciously utilized mutually planned and emergent approaches predicated on organizational change goals. In other words, organizations use whatever way is best to reach the desired end goals. Higgs and Rowland (2005) found that various change proposals fit well with multiple management methods. Change proposals also work well with a blend of planned and emergent approaches.

As the Central Jurisdiction created plans to wipe out the all-African American branch of the Church, they diagnosed that abolishing the Central Organization was only a bridge to reach more fundamental ends (Kirk, 2005). So, the Study Committee members who traveled to the conference came to help agree on what those ultimate end goals should be. They also were expected to help the Committee of Five decide the most practical and effective approaches for attaining the preferred ends.

Planned change is moving from Point A to Point B in a precise, structural way. This view denotes that the organization already understands its external environment and internal organizational culture and how it will react to the change. Interventions are put in place to respond to the anticipated changes so that organizations move smoothly to their next state.

Organizations utilize planned change to resolve challenges and crises, reexamine assessments, improve performance, influence future innovation, and enhance organizational effectiveness and competence (Cummings & Worley, 2008; B. Medley & Akan, 2008; Ven & Sun, 2011). Roberts (2017) emphasized that planned change is plans put into place preceding launching the objectives. It is a well-thought-out strategy. It is a deliberate choice to transform an organization's method of thinking, processing, and implementing.

Planned change is also a logical system, which resembles a step-by-step process to achieve the desired outcomes. This change process method is a deliberate approach to move organizations away from doing the same old thing the same old way and getting the same old results. To successfully implement a planned change process, leaders need to be open to "experimentation, improvisation, and the ability to cope with unanticipated consequences or repercussions" (Kerber & Buono, 2010, p. 181).

Also, planned change's success depends on the leadership and the entire organization sharing the same objectives during the change process (Burnes & By, 2012). Traditionally, organizations that formed healthy and principled work environments decreased their chances of being captured by a virus of peer pressure or climate of mistrust, creating resistance to planned change. Although planning change will alleviate some resistance, there may still be some opposition because of an assortment of other reasons.

Lewis, Laster, and Kulkarni (2013) conveyed that the process of change, as we would expect it to be, is contentious and divisive. Thus, the approach that leaders take to the change is vitally important. When organizational members misunderstand the need for change, their response will most likely be resistance. The hardness of heart will be the response from those members who think, "If it ain't broke, don't fix it." Some members are just stuck. They like the way things operate now, even if it is broken. These members enjoy the status quo.

Some members of organizations want to be a part of the change process. Executing change without notifying the people whom the change will affect can create unnecessary risk or more risk to the organization's central mission and vision (Leslie, Park, & Mehng, 2012). The threat to the organization's mission and purpose could emerge in various ways: low performance, increased resignations, an increase in transfers, and a toxic environment. If people, however, are allowed to engage in the change process, there is less resistance. Members will bowl you over with excitement about the change; full throttle as an engine will be their call of duty. So, by your organization permitting members to participate, it will generate more organizational commitment.

Some leaders prefer to have face-to-face meetings when there is a crisis, which creates further resistance because it adds more work to people's schedules (Dolan, 2011). Also, contacts, such as announcements and emails, that are not executed clearly during planned change can escalate employees' apprehension (Ye, 2012). Whenever you send emails, keep in mind that your emails do not allow enough facial expressions, and sometimes people can incorrectly perceive your voice tone. Emails can come across as demands when they are requests. So, planned face-to-face meetings allow for more clarification.

Weick (2000) stated that planned change has some advantages over emergent change. When observed inside the setting of large-scale organizational change, planned growth has the benefit of support from the people in power, who have the assets to focus on a clear, focused directive. Planned change also conveys to the stakeholders that the revamping is a well-constructed process.

Emergent Change Management

Emergent change is a continual process of experimenting with ideas and adjusting along the journey of organizational change. It is not deliberate but spontaneous and unwritten. The Central Jurisdiction Conference Study Committee was not a committee that the Methodist Church had established when the Church first considered eliminating the all-African American conference. The Church leaders created the Study Committee later to help process the multitude of proposals, recommendations, and divergent opinions the Committee of Five had to manage.

The emergent ideas that sprouted from the Study Committee as the Central Jurisdiction did its work helped formulate a document of statements and recommendations. These statements and recommendations empowered the African American region to speak with authority that Blacks within the Central Jurisdiction would serve together to fulfill their image of a Methodist Church consisting of people who came to Jesus in love and obedience. Black Methodists believed that this multitude of people who surrendered to the Lord are members of a new kind of community that transcends all cultural, racial, and class barriers (Kirk, 2005).

Although planned and emergent approaches are the two primary paradigms for achieving organizational change, planned change paradigms have ruled the corporate environment since the mid-20th century (Banford & Daniel, 2005). When it comes to managing change, organizations principally use the planned models because organizational leaders have become comfortable using these designs. Monetarily, organizations can manage projects more prudently and more cost-effectively. Furthermore, many leaders feel it is a waste of time to dive right into a project without planning because they believe that is a road to definite slow progress.

Nevertheless, regrettably, the bulk of organizational change endeavors utilizing planned models and tactics fail to accomplish their goals (Griffith, 2002). Gardner (2009) emphasized how planned change has become an island unto itself, but, if it is so vital to change, "why is it failing so much?" (p. 3)

Planned change is biased. It is just one side of the stream of consciousness. According to Barrett, Thomas, and Hocevar (1995), planned change paradigms and tactics highlight sensible planning and analysis and an undeviating order of steps. Planned change methods are characteristically deterministic. They assume a direct cause-and-effect connection between actions and outcomes. An intentional change point of view motivates organizational leaders to look for causes that will yield anticipated results. It is a global perspective that underscores design and control. It also supposes that an organization develops into what it becomes by way of logically and sensibly calculated systems and purposeful actions that leaders have decided to take.

Nonetheless, Weick (2000) proposed that planned change's language offers a one-sided interpretation of how to produce significant and productive change. It does not always evolve as planned. The intended plan may have said to go south, but unexpected variables interacted and determined that going northeast would be better for better outcomes.

Sometimes goals collide, bringing about an unintended result. When the company put its plan into practice, the approach gave the opposite calculation. The calculation may not be wrong; the result was just different. Therefore, focusing too much on planned outcomes is ill-advised.

Falconer (2001) posited that when organizations focus on planned results, they produce exceedingly low success rates by piloting organizational projects to precise intended outcomes. Falconer proposed that teams should instead concentrate on emergent change, learning lessons along their journey as the project progresses and develops rather than worrying about precise, established results. This type of planning Falconer described is more fluid and adaptive.

There is no predetermined process for changing organizations. It focuses on being responsive and adaptive to all environmental forces. The heart of emerging change assumes that change is continuously occurring, accommodating, and volatile. These occurrences make it necessary for organizations to adjust and readjust their values, chain of command, structure, and various other factors.

Your organization using this type of change—emergent—means your business will be more likely to manage change because of what naturally happens as your organization evolves. This type of change can also inspire meaningful change and compelling, productive organizational culture paradigm shifts throughout your organization. The growth will strengthen your establishment as a team. Your enterprise will also gain more innovative knowledge and set itself up for more collaboration from team members.

Similarly, Stacey (1996) argued that it is almost unachievable to establish shared purposes about long-term results among organizational members because organizations are multifaceted, progressing systems. Long-term effects, instead, emerge randomly from the ongoing collaborations of corporate members. Weick (2000) suggested that emergent change involves constant adjustments, adaptations, and revisions that yield necessary change without theoretical plans. Emergent change happens when people "re-accomplish routines and when they deal with contingencies, breakdowns, and opportunities in everyday work" (Weick, 2000, p. 237).

It seems that the factors that unleash resistance also cause failure. To mention a few, these failure factors are inadequate planning, inadequate communication, poor leadership, too many personal agendas, and a lack of flexibility. Any organization that seeks to change without thinking through the change process will encounter unrelenting resistance. Leaders who do not talk to organizational members whom the change will affect will produce destructive organizational behaviors. Leaders who do not garner support from the beginning of the change process will not receive the trust they need from corporate members. They will not convince members of the necessity for change.

If the organization has too many different objectives, it will be challenging to get buy-in from members. The organization may also make great plans, but new information arises once the organization implements the projects. This new knowledge may demonstrate that the organization should not be addressing the issue it set out to resolve but another problem. Instead of the organization adjusting, the organization continues full steam ahead.

All these factors lead to resistance and, ultimately, failure at the end of the change process. So, planned change is good for helping your organization be more efficient and productive, but there must be flexibility for emerging ideas. If your organization cannot adjust swiftly enough to preserve your business's reason for existing or adapt promptly to the changing ethos to keep the resources your establishment needs to stay alive, it will terminate itself; or your organization will become digested and incorporated into other organizations.

The Methodist Church exists today as the United Methodist Church because it could eventually see beyond its narrow, warped, and distorted church image. It became a new, more vibrant institution. It became a more inclusive and more productive team with more social power. Because the Methodist Church allowed ideas to emerge that changed its organizational culture, it became an effective instrument for mediating the gospel of Jesus Christ to the secular and irreligious organizations of our world (Kirk, 2005).

Equity Theory

Equity theory is built on the proposition that if members put in more than they are getting out of an organization, they will eventually become despondent. Organizations need to seek a fair balance between what they expect of their members and the rewards and incentives they give their members for their service. Otherwise, the relationship between the organizations and their members will be as fragile as a spider's web.

African American members who the Methodist Church forced into involuntary segregation and became known as Central Jurisdiction members always sought a fair balance. The equitable balance would help the Methodist Church blot out any of its policies against people of color. The just balance would not bar any people from worshipping in any Methodist Church because of race, color, or nationality. This fair balance would also ensure that the Methodist Church suture a healthy and productive relationship with all Methodist members, thereby laboring and delivering a unified Church. Because the Methodist practiced fair balance, this equitable practice would drive people toward the Methodist organization. People would feel the equality that they wept and cried out for.

John Stacey Adams, who was a workplace and behavioral psychologist, developed equity theory in 1963. It is one of the justice theories. Equity theory posits that subtle and variable factors impact employees' judgments and opinions about how they feel about their work and their coworkers (Adams, 1965). The theory proposes that if people think their organization is mistreating them, then they become apathetic. People may also become inattentive in their place of employment and with their fellow workers.

Some scholars and practitioners have described equity theory as inputs and outputs. Inputs are what people bring to organizations or situations. Those inputs could be education, experience, and skills. For example, Mr. Jones is a computer expert, and he brings his expertise to an organization, and he helps that organization improve and increase its income. That would be his input. The output would be how well the organization treats Mr. Jones and compensates him for his expertise (Schniederjans & Schniederjans, 2012). African Americans' motivations for a changed Methodist Church was that they wanted the Methodist organization to be open to all people. Through the years, African Americans had given their service diligently to the Church (input), but the Church still mistreated them (output).

For your organization to improve its performance, it needs to pay close attention to a fair balance. In other words, to increase your enterprise's efficiency, enhance your employee's tenure, and improve your member's satisfaction with your company, your business needs to have justice as one of its values. Fairness must be a mutual agreement between your organization and its members.

Expectancy Theory

In 1964, Victor Vroom developed the expectancy theory. Expectancy theory, sometimes called the expectancy theory of motivation, postulates that people's behavior is based on what they expect the reward will be for that behavior (Oliver, 1974). The Central Jurisdiction believed that their efforts to transform Methodism would give all of its members—Black and White—the opportunity to contribute to the Church's ministries.

African Americans believed whenever the Methodist organization gave people the chance to preach, teach, witness, or serve, the Methodist leadership should not base this privilege on people's color or race or nationality; the right for people to labor in the vineyard should be based on their skills, abilities, and knowledge of the Christian faith and Methodist traditions. They believed their efforts would erase the great anomaly and that membership in Christian ministry would be governed not by elitism and discrimination but inclusivity. These goals inspired them to charge up the exclusivity hills like a fire through the stubble.

Expectancy theory is the belief that people's efforts will produce their desired outcome. It is rooted in four hypotheses (Vroom, 1964). First, because people expect an institution to meet specific needs, they connect and unite with a particular organization (Lunenburg, 2011). The demand that an establishment fulfills impacts people's response to the organization. A second hypothesis is that people's behavior and performance are the results of deliberate choice. That is, people have the right to choose their responses based on their expectations.

A third hypothesis is that people are not all the same, so they want the organization to meet different needs (Vroom, 1964). For instance, some may wish for respect. Some may want more money. Others may desire job security. Fourth, the yearning to fulfill the need is intense enough to make reaching for the goal beneficial.

Expectancy theory highlights three antecedents: expectancy, instrumentality, and valence (Vroom, 1964). Expectancy has to do with people believing that exerting themselves will result in high performance. Instrumentality means that people think it is necessary to put forth a particular effort to procure a specific target or outcome. Lastly, valence has to do with people assessing the goals and products, which could be positive, neutral, or negative.

This valance stage simply means that when people have to decide between up, down, forward, or backward, they will select the response or choice that will give them the most valuable output or reward, as long as they see the prize as achievable. If the reward people want the most involves not obtaining it or is very risky, they will choose another course of action. The course of action they choose may not give them what they want but will provide them with something for their efforts. The all-Black area's members had a rock solid expectation that they would accomplish, with their joined forces, the objective to build an inclusive church.

Maslow's Hierarchy of Needs

Maslow's hierarchy of needs theorizes that people have to meet a specific criterion of needs before being whole and self-actualized. This process of obtaining wholeness and self-actualization requires starting with basic needs and then moving step by step up a pyramid. The result of racial exclusion in Methodism led to the founding of the following denominations: Colored Methodist Episcopal, African Methodist Episcopal, and African Methodist Zion Episcopal. People filled these denominations because they decided they could not reach their self-actualization in the MEC. However, for most African Americans, the right to belong, be accepted, and loved in a church in which so many African Americans and their ancestors responded to the Gospel message of Jesus Christ would not allow the sting of the scorpion of racism to paralyze their yearning.

Some African Americans who stayed in the Methodist Church became burned out after weathering so many racial storms. Nevertheless, despite the many attempts to marginalize them, they still hoped that they could become all God intended them to be in the Church. Maslow's theory postulates that people's needs, in the lower area of Maslow's pyramid hierarchy, must be met first before people can move up to the next level. The pyramid model levels are physiological, safety, love and belonging, esteem, and self- actualization. For example, to achieve love, safety must be completed first, and to reach self-esteem, people must first achieve love.

Psychoanalysis and behaviorism, which were part of the present doctrine, were inclined to emphasize problematic behaviors. Nevertheless, Maslow was much more concerned about learning about what made people happy and the things they did to reach their goals (Jerome, 2013). Maslow, who was a humanist, posited that people have a natural bend toward self-actualizing. They have the drive to become all they can become. The Black members who stayed in the Methodist organization despite discrimination felt they could fully utilize their God-given gifts within the Methodist fellowship. However, the factor that would facilitate this process was equality for Blacks in the Methodist structure.

Organizational Commitment

Despite the threat they received, African Americans' commitment to the Methodist Church was partly because of the service and sacrifices of those who had served before them. In 1758, John Wesley set the pattern for evangelizing, receiving, and discipling Black people by baptizing two slaves—one male and one female. After being baptized, these two people returned to Antigua and started a Methodist community (The People of the United Methodist Church, n.d.).

In Maryland, a Black woman named Anne Scheweiter in 1760 became one of the founding members of the first Methodist Society. Two years later, another Black woman known only by the name

Bettye visited Methodist services instituted by Phillip Embury in New York City. In 1768, when Methodist people built the John Street Church, several Black people's names appeared in the membership records. In 1784, Harry Hosier and Richard Allen, two nonvoting African Americans, attended the 1784 Christmas conference. This conference launched American Methodism (The People of the United Methodist Church, n.d.). Therefore, most African Americans felt that their allegiance to the MEC in the face of continually being ostracized was the right thing to do.

Porter, Steers, Mowday, and Boulian (1974) defined organizational commitment as the level of attachment people have toward a particular organization. Organizational commitment encompasses three aspects: (a) a strong dedication to the organization's goals and values, (b) a willingness to go the extra mile for the organization, and (c) an intense devotion to affiliated with the organization (Mowday, Steers, & Porter, 1979).

Another definition of organizational commitment that recurs is "an individual's psychological bond to the organisation, including a sense of job involvement, loyalty and belief in the values of the organisation" (O'Reilly, 1989, p. 17). Organizational commitment from this perspective means your corporate members accept your organizational goals. In conjunction with your members agreeing with your business's purpose, your members are eager to do more than required to make your enterprise a success (Lee & Miller, 2001).

Best (1994) stated that corporate members who have a high organizational commitment level act in a specific way. They will be loyal and devoted to the company for the good of the organization. These types of committed people believe it is the right thing to do rather than doing it only because there is something personal to be gained.

Self-Efficacy

Self-efficacy is people's conception that they believe they have the gifts, talents, or resources to accomplish a task (Bandura, 1977, 1986, 1997). It is the belief that one has the competence to command one's motivation.

During the 1960s conference, the Central Organization's delegates, in Cleveland, Ohio, voiced their dissatisfaction, discontentment, weariness, and anger. Instead of the Commission of Seventy making recommendations changing the Church's involuntary segregation laws, the Commission stunningly decided to sit on their hands. However, four years later, at the Seventh Quadrennial Session of the Central Jurisdiction, delegates' feelings were much more of a ray of sunshine. They had a brighter mood because, although at times it seemed like they were walking like blind people feeling their way, delegates had a feeling in their bones that they were in control of their destiny. "Part of this positive attitude was due to the Committee of Five's dedicated and imaginative work during the quadrennium from 1960-1964" (Kirk, 2005, p. 131).

People who think that they can accomplish a goal they set out to do are more likely to achieve the task (Bandura, 1997; Ross & Gray, 2006). These types of people can bring their goals from infancy to adulthood because of four reasons: (a) they set the challenging goals, (b) they do all they can to accomplish the purposes, (c) they believe they can achieve their plans do not give up because of obstacles and failures, and (d) they have principles that help them to deal with their emotional state of mind (Bandura, 1986; Gist & Mitchell, 1992).

Sasikala and Anthonyraj (2015) conducted a research project to identify the impact of employees' self-efficacy, emotional intelligence, and organizational commitment on resistance to change. The participants consisted of 77 manufacturing employees.

Sasikala and Anthonyraj (2015) utilized the convenience sampling technique to collect the data. Investigators used the following instruments to collect the data: Generalized Self-Efficacy Scale by Schwarzer and Jerusalem (1995); Assessing Emotions Scale by Schutte, Malouff, and Bhullar (2009); Organizational Commitment Questionnaire by Meyer, Allen, and Smith (1993); and Resistance to Change Scale developed by Oreg (2003). The findings indicated that all three—self-efficacy, affective commitment, and normative commitment—negatively relate to change resistance.

However, emotional intelligence and continuance commitment were not related to resistance to change among employees. Further, Sasikala and Anthonyraj (2015) showed the "relationship between self-efficacy and resistance to change reveals that when self-efficacy increases resistance to change decreases" (p. 32). When organizational leaders have high self-efficacy, it changes your leader's perception of their self-confidence. On the other hand, when your leaders have low self-efficacy, your leaders will not desire to lift a finger if the task is difficult or involves too many twists and turns. Bandura (1995) pointed out,

> People who have a low sense of efficacy in given domains shy away from difficult tasks, which they view as personal threats. They have low aspirations and a

weak commitment to the goals they choose to pursue. When faced with challenging tasks, they dwell on their deficiencies, the obstacles they will encounter, and all kinds of adverse outcomes rather than concentrate on how to perform successfully. (p. 11)

Low self-efficacy will pave the way for leaders toward behaviors that will cause them to throw in the towel; they will discontinue their pursuit of what is right for the organization. Low self-efficacy can also cause resistance to change (Satterfield & Davidson, 2000). The level of self-efficacy plays a role in any organization's ability to accomplish the transformation. From 1960 to 1964, the specific Central Jurisdiction members involved in surgically removing the racially segregated structure increased their belief in their ability to succeed. The work accomplished between 1960-1964 helped increase the Central Jurisdiction's well-being, self-confidence, reliance, and focus.

Transformational Leadership

Leaders who possess transformational leadership skills to stimulate, transform, and motivate others accomplish excellent results (Robbins & Coulter, 2007). These individuals do not shirk their leadership role. These types of leaders consider other people's developmental needs. They enable others to look at the latitude and longitude of circumstances and situations with fresh eyes. They also have the gift to energize people to give more than 100% toward achieving a particular goal.

Two years before the conference adopted Amendment IX, on April 25, 1956, a member of the Rock River conference, Harold A. Bosley, presented a six-point resolution that dealt with the Episcopal address. He argued that there was a need for the Methodist organization to see in a new light "the philosophy and effectiveness of the Jurisdictional structures of government begun seventeen years ago with the Unification of the three branches of American Methodism" (Thomas, 1992, p. 84). However, Bosley's resolution blatantly overlooked the Central Organization's racial structure. Chester Smith did not sit like a lamb and allow the glaring disregard to pass by unnoticed. Instead, he stood up and spoke against the resolution expressing that it was a hit below the belt for the General Conference to address the Methodist structure and not address the racially designed model—the Central Jurisdiction.

After Smith presented a well-conceived argument, the conference referred his resolution to the Committee on Conference Referral (Thomas, 1992). This referral did not do what Smith hoped it would do—get the proposal to the floor for further discussion. However, another member of the all-Black area, Thurman L. Dodson, was ignited by the room's emotions to speak, and he offered a resolution on segregation. It was also six points.

In his speech, Dodson declared that the General Conference from that day forward should not create any ministry model that marginalized and left in the cold any race or nationality. Furthermore, he stated that the General Conference should announce that any segregated system was out of step with Christian practice.

It became clear that day that the General Conference members had unutterable things pressing on their soul like a pent-up storm craving for an outlet. It also became clear on that day that they would not allow the conference to forget about the racial structure by sweeping it under the rug. Chester Smith motioned that the General Conference mandate that the Committee of the State of the Church develop and present a constitutional amendment that would terminate the Central Territory.

Your transformational leaders will be people who can inspire other people or groups in your establishment to take care of each other's needs and act in a way that benefits the whole group (Warrilow, 2012). James McGregor Burns (1978) introduced transformational leadership theory in his book, *Leadership*. B. M. Bass and J. B. Avolio extended the transformational leadership concept into organizational psychology and management (Jung & Sosik, 2002).

According to Hargis, Wyatt, and Piotrowski (2001), your transformational leaders will also be people in your institution who can enhance people's drive, self-confidence, performance, and morale. The way your transformational leadership will accomplish this feat is by attaining buy-in from corporate members. They will encourage members to take on more responsibility. Moreover, your transformational leaders will serve as role models for your organizational members. While transactional leaders influence people with rewards and punishment, transformational leaders influence people by their charisma. (Warrilow, 2012; Yukl, 2010).

Organizational Readiness for Change

Armenakis, Harris, and Feild (1999) explained that organizational readiness for change is the antecedent of whether people will resist change or support it. When businesses are ready for transformation, their new day is a little easier to bring to light. Armenakis et al. promulgated organizational readiness as the cognitive state involving attitudes, feelings, and behavior toward a change endeavor. Moreover, they claimed that when an organization is ready for change, resistance begins to disintegrate.

Several events led to the openness to change in the Methodist Church. Two of those events were the National Conference of the Methodist Youth Fellowship and the National attention. In 1941, during a National Youth Fellowship meeting, the youth adopted a resolution stating that they would organize to work against any form or fashion of racial segregation in the Methodist Church.

This group of young people, unbreakable as iron, lived up to their vows. Three years later, they popped the question: Is the Central Jurisdiction a racist structure? They proposed that the Methodist Church unplug the racial organizational system from the Methodist denomination's bureaucratic make-up. One of the other events that changed the proposition that a racially structured Church was right for Methodism was the momentum of the desegregation movement across America. As a result of the 1954 and 1955 Supreme Court's public-school decisions and the thousands of petitions to the General Conference requesting the elimination of the Central Jurisdiction, segregated attitudes and a stunning range of feelings began to show that changing the Methodist system was the order of the day.

Backer (1995) wrote that readiness is an organization's mental and emotional state of mind about doing something different. It is also the organization's belief that the company can achieve it. This mental and emotional state, Backer noted, is brought to fruition because the members of the organization believe that they are financially able to handle the change. They believe in the mission and leadership structure, and they believe the leadership team is cohesive and has the technical skills to transform the organization successfully for the better. At best, Bernerth (2004) suggested organizational preparedness affects the way the organization thinks. The organization is receptive and has confidence and the attitude to make the changes necessary.

Beer and Walton's (1987) definition of readiness, in their article "Organization Change and Development," is similar to Backer's (1995). They explained that preparedness is the collective, creative, or fundamental ability of a group or institution to give birth to a new process. Both Beer and Walton, and Backer suggested that readiness has to do with ability more than the organization's willingness. Jones, Jimmieson, and Griffiths (2005) defined readiness as organizational members having an optimistic view toward change because the change would be suitable for them and useful for the organization.

Cunningham et al. (2002) clarified that your organization's readiness consists of "a demonstrable need for change, a sense of one's ability to accomplish change (self-efficacy), and an opportunity to participate in the change process" (p. 377). V. D. Miller, Johnson, and Grau (1994) added that for your organization to be ready for a new day in the life of your business, your organizational members will need a high level of openness to change. As I studied organizational readiness's various definitions as well as the Methodist organization's definitions, I discovered several things. It is apparent to me that no matter what model you use—planned, emergent, or a combination of the two—your institution's new life is strongly connected to your organization's willingness to change, readiness to change, and commitment to readjust when necessary.

It is a required activity for you and your organization to understand the nuts and bolts of this chapter's words. It will clear the way for your business to understand organizational metamorphosis better. It will help your business, no matter what type it is, make sense of how turning things around is successfully produced so that you can get the best out of your corporate team.

You get the best out of people when you know how to get the best. Additionally, understanding the nuts and bolts of the words in this chapter will open the door for your business to give rise to a better workplace, better project outcomes, and better action and reaction to internal and external pressures. So, whatever stormy, foggy night your company is traveling through, grasping these terms in this section is one of the keys to brighter days ahead.

REVIEW QUESTIONS

1. What happens to an organization as a result of change?
2. If the shift in an organization is positive or negative, what happens? Explain both.
3. When people see an organization as an organism, how does it perform?
4. What does an organization need to perform effectively?
5. What does organizational culture mean?
6. List the various types of corporate cultures.
7. List the multiple factors that impact organizational culture.
8. What is the difference between planned change and emergent change? Which is better?

9. What is organizational commitment?
10. How do people demonstrate self-efficacy?
11. What is a transformational leader?
12. What does organizational readiness mean?

Chapter 2
CHANGE MANAGEMENT IN THE METHODIST ORGANIZATION

LEARNING OBJECTIVES

- Summarize the meaning of the debatable question.
- Discuss the one truth that your organization needs to keep in mind whenever it disagrees.
- Discuss the role Caucasian Methodists played in the racial tension in the United States.
- List some of the reasons Caucasians believed social equality between the Caucasians and the African Americans were unattainable.

- Explain the origin of the African Methodist Episcopal Church and the African Methodist Episcopal Zion Church.
- Discuss how planting a seed will help your organization to change and grow.
- Explain equity theory as it relates to the establishment of the all-Black area of the Church.
- Explain the expectancy theory as it relates to the establishment of the all-Black area of the Church.
- Discuss the various reasons some African Americans and Caucasians believed the Central Jurisdiction would be better for African Americans' future.
- Explain why African Americans were against a segregated Church.
- Discuss how providing space for people to challenge the status quo will help your organization.
- Discuss Bishop Thirkield's view on slavery and merging Caucasians and African Americans into the same Church.
- Summarize Joseph Lowery's speech that he gave on November 11, 1966.
- Explain self-actualization as it relates to the all-Black area of the Church.
- Discuss internal forces and how organizations should handle them.
- List some examples of external forces.
- Explain the ways that organizations can use external forces to change positively.
- Discuss three organizational change lessons that you learn in Chapter 2.

THE PEOPLE CALLED METHODISTS SHOULD NOT HAVE SEEN THE ideology that all people are born free like an issue that rose from obscurity, nor should it have been an epiphany, according to Bishop Woodie White, a retired bishop of the United Methodist Church. From the Methodist Church's beginning, there was uncertainty about race (W. W. White, 2009). This flaw was endemic during that time. This chapter continues to give a brief history of the Methodist Church between 1780-1968.

This chapter explores how the Methodist Church managed the change in society and the Church. It examines the debatable question: How should the Methodist Church handle the present and future circumstances of African American members. It focuses on multiple different ways the Methodist Church dealt with the Church's African American constituents. It also gives you organizational change leadership principles.

THE DEBATABLE QUESTION

As the Methodist Church continued to chart its way forward, the debatable question was still, "What do we do about the present and future circumstances of the African American members? What will be our relationship with them and their relationship with us?" (W. W. White, 2009). Some Caucasians saw it as a question and a problem that strangled the relationship between African Americans and Caucasians. When dealing with the debatable question, some Caucasian Methodists would often label the issue as "the Negro problem" or the "problem of the Negro" (Davis, 2008, p. 14).

Your organization will need to keep in mind that there are no problems that your organization cannot deal with as a team, and there are very few problems that your business will be able to solve divided. In every disagreement, your organization needs to commit to memorizing this truth: everyone who is a part of your organization is your partner. You all will either win the battles together or lose them together. Jesus said, "Every kingdom that fights against itself will be destroyed. And every city or family that is divided against itself will not survive" (Matt. 12:25, Easy-to-Read Version).

Bowen, who later was elected a bishop in the Church, proclaimed, "There is no such thing as a Negro problem . . . The real problem is the unwillingness of the White People of America to grant first-class and full citizenship to Negroes" (Richey, Rowe, & Schmidt, 2010, p. 390).

The mere question itself meant that the African American members were being subjugated and stigmatized. It denoted, in the words of Dr. Martin Luther King, Jr. (1986), that African Americans were being judged based on their color and not the content of their character. American Methodism spent "the next quarter-century debating this ecclesiastical apartheid and looking for a way to reorganize itself on a racially inclusive basis" (Richey et al., 2010, p. 388).

The debatable question, which was a contagious bacterial disease of injustice, plagued the Church and stirred up some within the Methodist collective conscience for a cure. Davis (2008) and McClain (1984) explained the reasons this debatable question agitated, motivated, and moved the collective consciences of some Methodists and would not go away: (a) promoting of American Christian patriotism, (b) advancing of White privilege, (c) strengthening Jim Crow, (d) maintaining a climate and culture of racial hatred, (e) preserving White superiority, (f) conflating the role of manhood for African Americans, and (g) protecting institutional unity.

Institutions' strategies are constructed on shifting sands, not solid rock, whenever they base their systems on the self-interest of privilege. Self-absorbed organizations only think about themselves. They plan and make decisions selfishly. They take actions selfishly. Respecting or regarding others is not in their sight. Then they wonder why they sink to the bottom of the sea like lead.

Some in the Church promulgated that American Christian patriotism and intensely fixed cultural racism were wedded (Davis, 2008). One could not be a patriot without also being a racist, and one could not be a racist without also being a patriot. Caucasian Methodists, analogous to the nation at that time, were terrified of miscegenation, profoundly worried about racial purity, and deeply worried about regulating social norms and, in particular, sexual restrictions between races.

Also, the debatable question would not go away because of the advancement of White privilege. Because many see Caucasian Christians as the majority race and because they held on to the most influential American religious institutions, there has also been a racial privilege perception. This White privilege has characterized the accepted wisdom on progress, civilization, and morality that has held dominance in American spiritual attitudes, theories, and ideas (Davis, 2008). Frankenberg (1993) posited that this prevailing whiteness frame of mind is a structural privilege, a place from which White people figure out themselves, others around them, and the global community.

In *Religion and the Rise of Jim Crow in New Orleans*, Bennett (2005) argued that Caucasian Christians played an expressive role in strengthening America's Jim Crow culture. Bennett explained that, in Caucasians yearning for a more united America, they, especially Methodists, urged and supported national identity formation intensely entrenched in a wholly racialized idea of citizenship. Caucasians wanted a national identity that stipulated that White is right. Kirk (2005) wrote that Southern Whites had a dim view of an inclusive church because such a church would destabilize and chip away at the Jim Crow system. And it would eventually weaken the legs of the present political and social structure.

Caucasian Methodists participated in maintaining a climate and culture of racial hatred. In *Rope and Faggot: A Biography of Judge Lynch*, W. White (2001) contended that much of the racial tension and hostility, which existed in the United States, could be attributed to Caucasian Methodists gravely fearing social equality between the races.

The majority of the Methodist Joint Commission confirmed on several occasions that they were obstinately against social equality—"black and white Americans eating together, chatting together, walking down the sidewalk together, and, if taken to the extreme, marrying and having children together" (Davis, 2008, p. 84). The committee presented several concepts, but the central idea that most of the Joint Committee could agree on was that social equality was at war with the Christian lifestyle. God made one race superior to all others, and the Lord never intended for the subordinate race to have the same status as the superior race.

Davis (2008) also elucidated that racial equality, racial unity, and Caucasian superiority in the Church continued to linger because Caucasians conflated the role of manhood for African Americans. Bederman (1995), in *Manliness and Civilization: A*

Cultural History of Gender and Race in the United States, 1880-1917, wrote Caucasians refined the discourse about civilization to a particular arrangement of tenets. This discourse involved three key factors: race, gender, and futuristic expectations about human developmental evolution. Some Caucasians believed that people had to achieve a particular state of manhood. Christian manhood was necessary for civilization to advance.

Christian men had to be strong and self-controlled. They had to be protectors of, and providers for, women, children, and their homes. The manhood of African Americans was degraded and diminished. Consequently, African American men were "placed farther back on the evolutionary scale of civilized progress than white men" (Davis, 2008, p. 15). Therefore, this meant that they did not deserve full manhood rights, which signified they did not merit full membership in the Methodist Church.

The Joint Commission even used African Americans' resistance to Caucasian unity to explain why the Methodist Church should not give African Americans full membership. The commission stated plainly and pointedly that the mere fact that African Americans were against the union between MEC and MECS without its African American members was a clear sign that Black people had not fully matured into Christian manhood. The debatable question continued to linger because Caucasians encouraged institutional unity instead of racial equality. Caucasians endorsed the White denominations' institutional integration as a more worthwhile sacred ideal than egalitarianism in the ecclesial realm.

As mentioned earlier, the themes led to the answer to the debatable question always being a proposal to create a separate structure for the African American members. The Chattanooga, Tennessee, Methodist contingency presented one such plan:

> The Colored Methodists would best be served through a union of all colored churches and members with the active financial and personal interests of the unified church... If the union of all colored churches cannot be secured, try a plan for union of the Colored Methodist Episcopal Church and the colored membership of the Methodist Episcopal Church. (Moore, 1943a, p. 91)

The race issue was still a thorn in the Methodist people's side. To be sure, Allen (1963) indicated, even though slavery had faded away, racial exclusion replaced it, and unification was intolerable without a settlement on the placement of Negro members. The Methodist people could not develop an integration plan to include African Americans in the whole Church that the South would approve. Every proposal led to an African American united church.

This plan, among other reasons, drove some Blacks away from the Methodist Church. These African Americans who left the Church created their own denomination—The African Methodist Episcopal Church and the African Methodist Episcopal Zion Church—and they were not about to reenter a church that refused to level the playing field. Therefore, without the stipulations to create a separate united African American faith or unit within the Methodist Church, a reunion was out of the question for them.

THE FORCES FOR THE STATUS QUO AND FORCES FOR CHANGE

When the Methodist Church separated African Americans into a separate jurisdiction, there was an immediate force of change to bulldoze the Central Jurisdiction and bring about a reunion (McEllhenney, Maser, Rowe, & Yrigoyan, 1992; Tuell, 2005). With the scent of the battle still on their clothes, members of the all-African American branch of the Church started making plans to undo the 1939 proposal. Even though the 1939 Uniting Conference's actions deeply wounded African Americans, African Americans still had a flicker of hope toward the future. W. W. White (2009) declared that during the first session of the newly formed all-African American territory, on June 18, 1940, members who were undiminished, confident, and unafraid. These sensibilities drove them to make two important commitments: (a) to be the most influential ministry leaders they could be and (b) to wipe out the all-Black division as early as possible.

Although the members knew it would be a long, challenging, and valiant struggle, they knew that they had to pressure the Church to abolish the Black area. The "members believed that such a structure was the shame of Methodism and an embarrassment in the larger community, especially in the black community" (W. W. White, 2009, p. 62). Kirk (2005) elucidated that African Americans planted seeds of reform that would take root and germinate a new inclusive church 29 years later.

There will be measures—thoughts, words, and actions—that your organization will take now that will be an act of planting a seed. These seeds will develop over time. For your organization to be successful, your leaders must understand that, the organizational seeds they plant now, they may never see the tree from that seed. Successful American business tycoon and philanthropist Warren Buffett (n.d.) stated, "Someone is sitting in the shade today because someone planted a tree a long time ago" (section 1). Your organizational members need to understand that some changes will not take root and bloom immediately. Some will bloom as the months and years pass.

We see equity theory at work in the elimination of the Central Jurisdiction. Here we apply it not to a person but a race of people. Equity theory focuses on whether or not a business fairly allocates the distribution of resources (Adams, 1963; see Chapter 1 for more on equity theory). The Methodist Church (force for the status quo) thought the African American jurisdiction was fair. Still, those in the African American jurisdiction (force for change) compared their membership entitlements to those of the Methodist Church entirely accepted into the Church.

The African American members concluded things were unequal. This decision affected the Central Jurisdiction members' motivation, behavior, and attitude. As a consequence of this frame of mind, the Central Jurisdiction stayed dissatisfied with the racially structured jurisdiction.

The all-African American jurisdiction members were not getting what they expected in a separate jurisdiction, and that was for the Church to treat them fairly and equally. We see, at this point, expectancy theory at work. With their exuberant nature and unswerving loyalty to the Methodist Church, the all-Black territory's members believed they could procure fairness and equity if the Methodist Church weeded out the all-African American segment of the Church. Expectancy theory purports that people are motivated when they feel their efforts will produce the rewards they seek (Vroom, 1964; see Chapter 1 for more on expectancy theory). Therefore, the desire to obtain dignity, acceptance, and equality motivated the Central Jurisdiction members to dismantle the Church's portion based on race.

Forces for the Status Quo

Some Blacks, who were internal influencers, were against the merger. They were lukewarm about the union because they thought Amendment IX would financially weaken the Central Jurisdiction. According to W. W. White (2009), this is why some Central leaders discouraged the most vibrant churches from transferring to the White conferences and jurisdictions. Like Melvin Talbert (who later became a UMC bishop), some were against the merger because they felt the EUB was receiving more guarantees than the Black jurisdiction.

Others' opinions were that the Central structure allowed Blacks to choose their leaders. The new merger structure would dilute Blacks' power to choose their own bishops, district superintendents, department heads, and other leaders. In the new church, Whites would outnumber Blacks and would always be the deciders. Agreeing to merge, African Americans would be putting the selection of Black leadership in White people's hands.

Others (Caucasians and Blacks) thought the Central Jurisdiction was the perfect system that the African American Methodist members needed to develop their leadership. Why? It united African Americans across the span of the Church. It was growing into a coast-to-coast empowering organization that afforded recognition, advancement, selection, training, and preparation of African American leaders (Davis, 2008; Irvin, 1992; McClain, 1984; Richey et al., 2010; Thomas, 1992).

The Black area also gave national attention to the various African American colleges and universities, such as "Bennett, Bethune-Cookman, Claflin, Clark, Dillard, Gammon Theological Seminary, Meharry Medical, Morristown, Paine, Philander Smith, Rust, Samuel Huston, and Wiley" (Richey et al., 2010, p. 389). In *The Jurisdictional System*, Bishop Short (1964) wrote,

> While it is true that the Central Jurisdiction has become a symbol of segregation, and as such must be apologized for, it is also true that it has brought to the Negro certain guarantees in the total life of the church, which he did not have prior to union, and which he has greatly valued, and which have enriched both him and the total life of the church. (p. 5)

In *Breaking Down the Walls: A Contribution to Methodist Unification*, Cranston (2011) argued that it was in African Americans' best interests to have their own separate church. He contended that African American men should have the title of men. They were qualified to have complete residency in God's kingdom because they had demonstrated themselves creditable for God to bestow on them manhood, faithfulness, and courage.

Although the statement seems mind-boggling and wildly off the mark, Cranston (2011) asserted that African Americans had *manhood-consciousness* and freedom to determine their destiny because

Caucasian Methodists had vested them with it. Nevertheless, although African Americans were men in God's eyes, they were not wholly of manhood status in the Church. African American men were making progress. Nonetheless, they were quite far away from full manhood in the Church, which meant that they were incapable of managing church governance duties on a large scale.

Moreover, Cranston (2011) postulated that it was up to African Americans to grow and learn to take on more church responsibilities. He suggested that segregation was the best way for African Americans to accomplish this goal. Mixed-race denominations or mixed-race churches not only would hinder this progress but also would prevent African Americans from procuring the type of African American pastors they would prefer.

In *The South Today*, one of John Moore's (1943b) premises for keeping the Church segregated was his belief that African Americans were still a *child race*. They needed assistance from the adult Caucasian race to mature. Therefore, in Moore's view, African Americans becoming fully matured adults was impossible. Because African Americans could not develop much in economics, intelligence, and social development, they would only contribute to their race.

Like an echo without a voice, they would be unable to add much to the broader religious influence of Caucasian Methodists. Therefore, it was not in the best interests of Caucasian Methodists for African Americans to be integrated into the Church. Besides, several White people believed that an integrated church was not advantageous for Caucasians or African American Methodists.

As you reorganize your business, be sure to create space for your leaders, members, and partners to challenge the status quo.

Lessons from the Methodist Reformation that Will Transform Any Organization

The most successful companies are those that sail the seas of time requesting new perspectives. What is the next big thing for your company? Is what you are doing working? Maybe you are saying you do not know. Well, as you reprioritize, now is the time to create a culture where you no longer manage the status quo but manage recreating growth.

Forces for Change

Internal forces for change. Schein (1990) noted that individual organizations have forces within, such as unions, leadership styles, and leadership and employee relationships, that direct, shape, and characterize organizational culture. In the Methodist organization, internal forces were triggering the Methodists to change. These voices varied from individuals to groups.

African American Methodist leaders made substantial contributions to the Methodist structural changes. Daily, they sought to steer the Methodist Church toward a genuine community. Daily, they strove to move the Church away from being bonded by race and superiority toward being bonded by equality, justice, and agape love.

The all-Black territory's members and some progressive Caucasians adamantly disagreed with the premise Caucasians and African Americans would be best served by segregating African Americans into their own branch of Methodism. Although at times, it seemed like their spirits beat themselves like cage birds against their prison bars of injustice in vain, Blacks never absorbed the racist climate and pernicious propositions about their ancestral make-up.

They never yielded the right-of-way to the negative judgments framed about them or an integrated church. Unfailingly, they believed in a God who created them to have every opportunity to go wherever their interest and talents led them. Some churches exist today because African American Methodist leaders refused to permit the Methodist Church to marginalize them.

As early as 1787, Methodist African American leaders such as Richard Allen protested and resisted White supremacy in the Church. In anguishing detail, Richard Allen illustrated this scene of the protest and resistance in this way:

> We had not been long upon our knees before I heard considerable sculling and low talking. I raised my head up and saw one of the trustees H— M—, having hold of the Reverend Absalom Jones, pulling him up off his knees, and saying, "You must get up—you must not kneel here." Mr. Jones replied, "Wait until prayer is over." Mr. H— M— said, "No, you must get up now, or I will call for aid and force you away." Mr. Jones said, "Wait until prayer is over, and I will trouble you no more." With that he beckoned to one of the other trustees, Mr. L— S— to come to his assistance. He came and went to William White to pull him up. By this time prayer was over, and we all went out of the Church in a body, and they were no more plagued with us in the Church . . . My dear Lord was with us, and we were filled with fresh vigor to get a house erected to worship God in. (Mays & Nicholson, 1933, p. 44)

Eventually, those who were part of this event left the Church. Still, they contributed to the change that would transpire within the Methodist denomination, abolishing the all-Black conference. However, there were African American leaders who did not leave; they formed groups and worked individually to oppose the hideous experience of racism, marginalization, and White supremacy in the Methodist structure. They also had a profound impact on the organization and relationships in the Methodist Church.

They assiduously worked to defend and preserve what little rights African Americans had. From the historical record, it is evident that the leaders who eventually left the Church, and groups such as the Committee on the State of the Church were an internal force for change unaltered by antagonisms.

The Black jurisdiction members never saw themselves as genetically inferior or culturally weak. In its report to the 1956 General Conference, the Committee on the State of the Church took a strong stance against segregation in the Church by expressing that the Lord's teachings prohibited discrimination. The chairperson of the committee, Charles C. Parlin, declared that the world was watching the Methodist General Conference awaiting what decisions it would make about the racial issue. He said that a message had come to him stating that the Republican and Democratic parties were drafting policies to address the country's racial problems. Nevertheless, the Republicans and Democrats were waiting to see what the Methodist voices had to say about this issue ("General Conference of 1956," 1956; Thomas, 1992).

The following associations were other groups who were internal forces for change: Methodist college and university students and faculty, the "unofficial Methodist Federation for Social

Action (MFSA), the Methodist Student Movement (MSM), and the Women's Division of the Board of Missions and its local affiliate, the Women's Society of Service (WSCS)" (Richey et al., 2010, p. 391), and other Methodist members. Methodist colleges and university students and faculty pushed administrations and trustees to integrate (Richey et al., 2010). In *Sweet Land of Liberty: The Forgotten Struggle for Civil Rights in the North*, Sugrue (2008) highlighted that educators at Drew University appealed to the General Conference to wipe off the map the all-Black jurisdiction.

Charles Webbers, the new leader for the Methodist Federation for Social Action, sought to convince "the church's publishing house to sign a contract with the printing trades" (Richey et al., 2010, p. 391). At the Methodist Building in Washington, Webber endeavored to integrate the dining hall. To clarify that it was against any segregation in the Church, in 1948, the Methodist Federation for Social Action elected African American Bishop Robert Brooks as its president.

From its inception, the Methodist Student Movement disavowed racial segregation by establishing itself as an organization with no racial obstacles and adopting principles that emphasized racial understanding. The Methodist Student Movement included the dean of the chapel of Fisk University, W. J. Faulker, as a conference leader. The Methodist Student Movement National Council included student representatives from the Central Jurisdiction. There was also an expressed appeal that all student leaders should be determined to work for understanding, cooperation, and collegiality on every level of the Church. The Methodist Student Movement National Council also conveyed that all student leaders should work for the day when the Methodist Church could integrate and come together as one Methodist people.

The Women's Division proactively sought to bring the Methodist Church out of the wilderness of segregation through its employment and meeting policies (Keller, Ruether, & Cantlon, 2006; Sugrue, 2008). In 1941, Charlotte R. French was the first African American secretary hired in the New York office. In 1948, Theresa Hoover was elected the first African American senior staff person. The Women's Division would not have any meetings at any place that practiced racial segregation and did not welcome all its members (Richey et al., 2010).

Your organization will need policies that match your behavior and behaviors that fit your guidelines. For your organization to be successful, your vision, value, and culture cannot be enemies. They must speak the same language and demonstrate the same demeanor. Once these policies are positioned, enforcing these guiding principles is vital to your organization's continual growth and progress. Your organization will start to lose integrity when these three components do not match.

The Secretary of the Southern Jurisdiction Department of Christian Social Relations and Local Church Activists of the Women's Division, Dorothy Rogers Tilly, was a stellar example of a justice organizer. She organized Caucasian women and African American women to fight against racism in the Church and community (Houck & Dixon, 2009; Richey et al., 2010). Tilly fought to disable racism wherever it reared its ugly head. She was an antilynching activist and asked other women to get involved in the antilynching movement. History has shown that Tilly stood in front of a Mississippi lynching mob and refused to let them pass. Also, in Georgia and South Carolina, she played an active role in organizing against the Ku Klux Klan.

After the landmark United States Supreme Court case *Brown v. Board of Education of Topeka* decision that declared state laws creating separate public schools for African American and Caucasian students unconstitutional, more support came for removing racial structures. The Women's Society of Services and the new EUB, two other internal forces for change, also demonstrated their support against segregation in any form or fashion, applauded the court's decision. They also renewed their commitment to exterminate segregation. The Women's Society of Services stated,

> We affirm anew our determination to work with greater urgency to eliminate segregation from every part of our community and national life and from the organization and practice of our own church and its agencies and programs. We rejoice that the highest tribunal in this land, the Supreme Court of the United States, proclaimed on May 17, 1954 that segregation in public education anywhere in this nation is an infringement of the Constitution and a violation of the Fourteenth Amendment.
>
> We accept our full Christian responsibility to work through church and community channels to speed the process of transition from segregated schools to a new pattern of justice and freedom. (The *Methodist Woman* as cited in Richey et al., 2010, p. 393)

Specific individuals who were internal forces of change, such as Chester A. Smith, thunderously defended the Black territory's position. He expressed in 1956 that the Methodist Church needed to deal with the 350,000 African American Methodist members whom the Church had segregated because of their ethnicity ("General Conference of 1956," 1956; Thomas, 1992). He said that segregation in the Methodist Church was a deplorable practice and policy that the Church needed to discontinue and build a nonracial structure.

To support his argument, Smith highlighted an external force, the Supreme Court's recent decision concerning the public schools. In that case, *Brown v. Board of Education of Topeka*, the Supreme Court ruled that separate educational facilities were fundamentally unequal, overruling the *Plessy v. Ferguson* ruling (C. E. Lincoln, 1967; Rubin, 2016). African Americans did not see integration as a foe but as the remedy, the method to drive a stake into the heart of racial policies in the Church. They felt they had earned a right to be at the table.

In 1963, there were five African Americans and two Methodist Bishops, James Matthews (Caucasian) and Charles Golden (African American), who challenged the racial segregation policies of Galloway Memorial Methodist Church (Matthews, 2000; Richey et al., 2010). In 1961, the Galloway board members approved a formal resolution barring the entrance of any person the greeters or ushers deemed a threat to peace by trying to defy the Galloway Memorial racial segregation policy.

Two years later, the board strengthened its guiding principle, specifying they desired to have an all-Caucasian church membership (Richey et al., 2010) forever. The custom of racial segregation in the Galloway Memorial Methodist church was a long-established practice (Matthews, 2000). Five African Americans decided to test those guiding principles, which led to "the resignation of the pastor and the Associated Press coverage of his sermon protesting the exclusion" (Richey et al., 2010, p. 396).

Several other ministers, including Bishop James Matthews and Bishop Charles Golden, continued the protest against the Galloway segregation policy. Bishop Matthews and Bishop Golden, along with seven other ministers, went to Galloway Memorial and asked to be seated. The seven ministers were arrested and jailed for trespassing (Matthews, 2000; Richey et al., 2010). The internal forces of change also existed among the Council of Bishops. At the Council of Bishop's meeting in Detroit in November 1964, the Council presented a noteworthy declaration, appealing for racial inclusiveness in all Methodist churches:

> The Methodist Church stands for equal rights of all racial, cultural and religious groups. We confess with deep penitence that our performance as a church has not kept pace with our profession. The right to choose a place of residence, to enter a school, to secure employment, to vote or join a church, should in no way be limited by a person's race or culture. The Methodist Church must build and demonstrate within its own organization and program a fellowship without racial barriers. ("Church Segregation," 1964, p. 3)

Your organization can learn all about organizational structure and chain of command, but if it does not realize that it takes leaders to lead the way to inspire people to want to change, very little will be accomplished. Change leaders want their companies to wake up different, and they can achieve change by getting others to enlist in the evolution and adapt to the various phases of the growth.

Throughout the Methodist Church's history, as it sought to deal with racial segregation, there have been internal forces, brimming with confidence, seeking to navigate the harsh racial landscape to guide, shape, and brand the Methodist Church's organizational culture into an inclusive denomination.

Robert Elijah Jones, a prime mover in Methodism, presented several reasons for integration. According to Davis (2008), Jones had a considerable impact on the idea of union. Jones presented

> several arguments in favor of a merger plan in which African American and Caucasian Methodists were members of the same church, but segregated by conference—essentially laying out the basic plan that would be implemented more than twenty years later. (Davis, 2008, p. 32)

Bishop Thirkield wrote that slavery was in God's plan. He believed that a new inclusive church would conclude in the complete integration into one Methodist Church. He made it public that he thought that all of the people who were the offspring of slaves, after being integrated into the Caucasian Methodist Church, would be a step closer to becoming an utterly civilized race (Davis, 2008). Thirkield felt that slavery and the One Church plan—Caucasian and African Americans in one Church—were all working according to God's divine strategy.

Henry Nelson Snyder, President of Wofford College (1902-1942), also advocated for an inclusive church. Although he felt it was a plan that the Church should propose and implement, he thought it would fail. He believed that even after the Methodist Church integrated African Americans into the Church, they would never truly feel welcomed. Bringing the races together was worth the try, but it would never work. America would never be a home for former Africans, no matter how much Caucasians tried to include them and how much former Africans tried to feel at home in their new world (Davis, 2008).

In 1958, when the Church affirmed it would use Amendment IX to deal with local church transfers, although some thought it was being put in place to make racial structural change difficult, at that time, only a White woman named Thelma Stevens stood up and spoke against the Amendment. She argued that Amendment IX was only a process to get rid of a visible racial structure. However, Amendment IX was not a plan for the Church to actively work to provide every racial group the "opportunity without discrimination to enjoy full participation in all activities of the Church" (Kirk, 2005, p. 43). Her opinion was that the amendment was unequivocally too narrow.

On November 11, 1966, Lowery, with consummate communications and leadership skills and with his formidable persuasive powers, delivered an eloquent appeal to end segregation and expressed his belief in an inclusive Methodist Church. As he spoke, the Central Jurisdiction members—and others—lit up with approval, nodded their heads, and shouted "Amens." Lowery was always collegial in his approach:

> Mr. Chairman, and members of this historic General Conference, I think it is indeed an historic conference, because we face an exciting parallel between the Conference and the union that we—the new beginning that we had in 1939 and 1949, and the possible new beginning in 1966 and 1968.
>
> At that time, as we had that new beginning, we embraced racism in the life and structure of our church. We voted against a motion of reconciliation made on Calvary by the Lord of the Church. And we deleted that motion, and erected walls of separation in terms of Annual and Jurisdictional Conferences. And after 26 long years, those walls still separate us. (Lowery, 1966, p. 851)

As he stood among his peers and those who were adamantly against what he stood for, Lowery waxed eloquently with his words as he often did when he spoke. He wanted to know why the walls of racism had been built and not torn down. Jude, who some people believe was the brother of Jesus, reminded the Church that the Lord called the Body of Christ to bring people together, not cause division.

Jude brought to light to the Church the things that Jesus said: In the end, there will be people who are not sincere about brotherly and sisterly love and unity. "They'll treat them like a joke and make a religion of their own whims and lusts. These are the ones who split churches, thinking only of themselves. There's nothing to them, no sign of the Spirit" (Jude 1: 18-19, The Message). As Jude said to the Church in his day, Lowery said to the Methodist

Church, if anyone should know about the Lord's call for esprit de corps among his followers, it should be the Church. Lowery asked the Church,

> Was God wrong? What is wrong with the children of God whom God has chosen to hue with color, that we continually reject them and their fellowship and our reconciliation with them in the name of our risen Lord?
>
> How long must we wait for a favorable and affirmative vote on that motion?
>
> Is there something wrong with us? If we are discriminated against because we are unclean, we wash. "Is there something wrong with us?" (Lowery, 1966, p. 851)

Lowery told those who constructed barriers against integration that African Americans would do whatever was required to break down the walls of inequality in the Church. But there was one thing that African Americans could not do—change the color of their skin. The answer, however, is not changing the hue that God colored Black people. The answer is to change the Church's out-of-tune voice that God did not create all people equally—that some people are rightfully the master of other people by birth.

In the words of Professor Eddie Glaude (2016), this is a mask, and we must remove it to call attention to White advantage. Only then will we stand any chance whatsoever to understand each other better, free ourselves from the shackle of fears about unity, and slay the stereotypes about Black people. Bennis (2009) said, every great inventor or scientist has had to unlearn conventional wisdom in order to proceed with his or her work. For example, conventional wisdom said, 'If God had meant man to fly, He would have given him wings.' But the Wright brothers disagreed and built an airplane (p.66).

True change involves unlearning habits and conventional wisdom that confine us to mediocrity and paradoxes. (Bennis, 2009). Lowery (1966) continued to present his case for inclusivity:

> If we are discriminated against because we are ignorant, we seek to learn. If we are discriminated against because we are loud or boisterous, we seek to be refined and intelligent.
>
> But, if we are rejected on the basis of our color, we are helpless, because God made us black, and there is nothing we can do about it.
>
> And so, we appeal to this Conference in the name of what may be the last opportunity at this historic session to make a witness, a universal witness in this today, and approved a motion that Christ made when he died. (p. 851)

Lowery reminded the Church that what African Americans were asking for was a sine qua non of African Americans and a sine qua non of God. Blacks felt that their requirement was a divine requisite. Jesus prayed,

> I am not praying just for these followers. I am also praying for everyone else who will have faith because of what my followers will say about me. I want all of them to be one with each other, just as I am one with you and you are one with me. I also want them to be one with us. Then the people of this world will believe that you sent me. (John 17:20-21, Contemporary English Version)

Lowery (1966) told the Church the Lord resolved the race problem a long time ago:

> We ask you to settle an issue that has already been settled on the actor's stage, on the athlete's field, and on the dancer's pavilion. It's been settled in the beer drinker's saloon, but it has not been settled at the altar beneath the Cross of Jesus, where it was settled so long ago. (p. 851)

For some, it was hoped that Amendment IX would help dissolve the all-African American body of the Church by 1976. But Central members like W. Astor Kirk did not want to take that chance. Kirk decided to present an amendment, known today as the Kirk amendment, specifying that the Church's Constitution not include the Central Jurisdiction system. This amendment was confirmed 464 to 362.

Although Kirk's amendment passed, the Methodist Church's southern leaders still wanted to hold on to the racial structure, arguing before the Judicial Council that it was their right to structure their conference however they saw fit. Steeled by his conviction, Kirk presented his rationale why he and others opposed the southern leaders' stance. The council ruled in Kirk's favor.

Caucasians who thought that the Black Jurisdiction was needed to produce influential Black leaders and Blacks in the Central Jurisdiction who thought otherwise did not have kindred spirits when it came to the separate-but-equal philosophy. Between Caucasians and African Americans, there was an immense gulf about the Church's future.

People in your organization will have various opinions about change and how your institution should approach it. Some views

> will be like a sharp knife. There are foolish people who regard it only with terror, and dare not touch or meddle with it; there are more foolish people, who, in rashness or defiance, seize it by the blade, and get cut and mangled for their pains; and there are wise people, who grasp it discreetly by the handle, and use it to carve. (Wilstach, 1916/2010)

Some people will want to be pushy about the change. No plan. "Let's just decide what we want to do and tell everyone this is how it is going to be done and do it." Some people will say, "if it ain't broke, then don't fix it." Others will say that the entire system needs overhauling. The opinions about what needs to happen to improve your business's performance will be as many as the stars. This organizational evolution is why it is such a tedious task to get right. Therefore, your organization needs to understand the best practices for change management, which I highlight in this book.

African Americans presented theological and biblical reasons that the Methodist Church could not tolerate segregation in the Church. Contrarily, Caucasians gave theological and biblical basis that doctrinal and scriptural motives were not germane to the integration concept (Davis, 2008). African Americans felt like they could not feel like complete members of the Methodist Church and reach their full potential as long as the Church excluded them from full participation. The Church, a majority of the African Americans felt, was created to make people whole.

The Central Jurisdiction's members saw their membership status, their change, and their self-actualization hinged on being full-fledged Church members. So, it is understandable, according to Maslow's hierarchy of needs theory, why the Central Jurisdiction's members could not reach self-actualization (Dunmore, 2013). Maslow posited that there are five stages of condition: (a) physiological needs—air, food, drink, and shelter; (b) safety needs—protection, safety, and order; (c) love, relationship, and belonging needs; (d) esteem needs; and (e) self-actualization needs. The first stage relates to physiological needs. People cannot go to the next step until they feel fulfilled in their present location (see Chapter 1 for more on Maslow's theory).

Once a group of people feels that their organization has met the group's needs, they can move to the next stage, which would be safety. In the Central Jurisdictional case, the Methodist Church's racial policies hampered the members' progress. Why? Because they could not move to the stage of love, relationship, and belonging. In other words, they could not move beyond their present state of mind until members felt that the Church loved them—until they belonged and the Methodist Institution welcomed

Lessons from the Methodist Reformation that Will Transform Any Organization

them with open arms. Wanting to be accepted, wanting to be loved, is why they fought profusely against the system, the cage in which they felt trapped. Thus, they relentlessly scuffled for change and eradication of the all-Black conference.

As your organization considers the changes it wants to make, you will need to keep at the top of your list how you want your team members to feel as you progress along your change journey. If you want them to think that they belong, you have to put things in place to help them feel that way. You can make sure you have members from every level of your company on the change team. Another thing you can do to accomplish this goal of belonging is to ask them what changes they want to see. Remember, when your members do not feel like they belong, they will revert to what Maslow calls safety level. They will seek to protect their space instead of collaborating and creating more efficient and just ways to operate.

The pressure compelled the Methodist organization to begin to initiate ways to end the racial structure. As early as 1944, the Methodist Church felt the death rattle of its segregated system. As a result, the denomination decided to find ways to eventually abolish racial injustice in the Church by establishing a task force to "consider afresh the relations of all races included in the membership of the Methodist Church" (Thomas, 1992, p. 74).

In 1948, the Central Jurisdiction established its own task force, its own internal influencers to study the Church's all-African American branch. The specific purpose of the Central Jurisdiction study task force was:

> With a vision to play an active role in eradicating the Central Jurisdiction, the Central Jurisdiction

commissioned a study group also to study itself. Its purpose follows: The purpose of this Commission shall be to study the Central Jurisdiction with a view to determining its advantages and its disadvantages; its relationship to other Jurisdictions; its overlapping boundaries, problems arising out of its extensive geography; its status as a racial group in the Methodist Church, and any other problems peculiar to the Jurisdiction. This study shall have as its purpose the establishment of an intelligent basis for determining whether or not the Central Jurisdiction should be continued as it now exists or eliminated, and what modifications, if any, should be made, and the steps necessary to make such modifications. (Thomas, 1992, p. 75)

This internal force's objective would be to make a statement that African American Methodists would play a key role in their membership change status and self-actualization by helping to unravel the cultural quandary.

The organizational change lesson. The lesson that should be learned from this is that internal forces will be beneficial to your corporate change process. Examples of internal forces are people, events, structures, systems, and environments. If your employees are always complaining about work conditions, salaries, interpersonal relationships, and leadership styles, do not continue to ignore these complaints. These internal forces can make or break your company.

These internal influencers can cause your business to become extinct or improved. Many organizations fail to reach their goals because they silence these voices. Do not do that. Instead, find a way to collect these data from your internal movers and shakers and utilize it to improve your performance. When your internal forces feel good and reach their personal goals, so will your company.

External forces for change

The process of changing African Americans' membership status and self-actualization in the Methodist Church by eliminating the Black Jurisdiction (a symbol of segregation) did not start within the Church; it began with forces of change from outside the denomination. Eternal forces pressured the Church to evolve. The first Freedom Riders compelled the Church to look at its race problem. Jackie Robinson joined the Brooklyn Dodgers to play baseball, and several other societal changes helped the Methodist Church to understand culture was attacking segregation's empire. The result would be discrimination would come tumbling down (Thomas, 1992). Feeling these attacks and seeing the walls of segregation crumbling, the Methodist Church saw Methodist presence in its current form as an eyesore and a contradiction.

The external forces that were generating change in the Methodist Church's structure—leading to the Black conference's removal—were the societal changes taking place in the United States. As Bishop Woodie White (2009) so profoundly said,

> There always has been the interconnection between culture and religion. Sometimes religion has impacted

the culture, and more often than not, the culture has impacted religion. Still, one cannot think of the development of religion apart from the culture in which it exists" (p. 58).

The pressure for change was gaining momentum. Change was taking place all across America. External influencers were unlocking doors to the narrow confinements placed on African Americans' opportunities and aspirations; that change influenced Methodists' attitudes.

James Farmer, who was African American, and George Houser, who was Caucasian, both graduate students of the Methodist University of Chicago, initiated the Congress of Racial Equality in 1942 (Davis, 2008; Frazier, 2017; Meier & Rudwick, 1973). They used this new organization to conduct the first sit-ins, which demonstrated against discrimination in Chicago restaurants.

Later, the Congress of Racial Equality would propel the first Freedom Riders to test compliance with the 1946 Supreme Court decision that interstate travel segregation was unconstitutional. In 1946, President Harry Truman established the President's Committee on Civil Rights to examine civil rights conditions in the United States. He submitted recommendations that would improve these rights.

The Supreme Court had begun to explore the question, "What is the meaning of equality in the concrete life of the American people" (Quarles, 1987, p. 236). From 1938-1950, the courts began to test the theory of *separate but equal* (Goldstone, 2011; McEllhenney et al., 1992; K. Medley, 2012). The courts ordered the University of Missouri to admit African Americans to law school.

In 1947, the government desegregated the armed forces. In 1955, the police arrested Rosa Parks for refusing to vacate her seat on a bus, which led to the Negro boycott of the Montgomery, Alabama, bus system (Haskins, 1999; C. E. Lincoln, 1967). During the 1960s, Dr. Martin Luther King, Jr., was traveling all over the country—and the world—talking about a dream he had that would bring people together across racial boundaries, crumble the walls of segregation, and dissipate the hatred people had for one another.

The EUB played a major role in abolishing the Central Jurisdiction. By 1964, the EUB and the Methodist Church were discussing merging the two denominations. The EUB was not a segregated church. To achieve merge between the EUB and the Methodist Church, the EUB stipulated that the Methodists had to dispose of their segregated policies.

A mood of reform was pushing its way across America, bringing unbearable strain on Methodism. The external environment in which the Methodist Church existed was changing, and it began to move, persuade, and compel the Church in a new direction. Amid the momentous changes occurring in American society, the forces of stability that protected the status quo were being overwhelmed and overrun by the forces of change. Those external forces impacted the Methodist Church's Council Bishop's address, leading to the most precise and firmest statement the Methodist Church had ever made against the Central Jurisdiction.

One of the Church's bishops presented that statement in the Episcopal address:

> We are dedicated to the proposition that all men are created equal, all men are brothers, and all men are

> of eternal worth in the eyes of God. Prejudice against any person because of color or social status is a sin . . . We believe that this General Conference should insist upon the removal from its structure any mark of racial segregation and we should do it without wasting time. ("Episcopal Address," 1964, p. 15)

Voices across the country were broadcasting that no one should be a second-class citizen, scorned and disregarded, especially in the Church.

The organizational change lesson. The lesson here is that internal forces will be helpful to your organization and external influencers. External movers and shakers will also help your business learn what it needs to be successful and what it needs to discard. Examples of these external forces are customers, technology, competition, resources, and social and political environments. Technology such as Facebook and Zoom have helped to extend our reach. Any size company can be a global business at the push of a button. External forces can be a tremendous incentive to determine your organization's day-to-day decisions and future actions for a better future.

Do not fight against these forces. Use them to your advantage to make your company more fruitful. The result will be that your organization's weaknesses will not continue to diminish your company's effectiveness.

Methodists had a weakness that caused their body to be sick. External forces brought to light that the Church had to inoculate against the Church's disease of exclusivity. The pathogens that triggered this disease came in various forms: racism, White nationalism, race consciousness, and White supremacy.

To rid the Church of the disease, the Methodist organization had to treat the pathogens by helping a considerable number of Caucasian brothers and sisters understand that all of God's children should be empowered, engaged, and involved in the whole life of the Church and not excluded because of race. At first, the status quo did not want to hear the cure, but eventually, the voices who desired a new day opened the Church's ears. The forces of change—both internal and external—had to clarify that a segregated Church is a relic of White racism, and the Body of Christ must abolish racial prejudice in all of its forms (Davis, 2008; McClain, 1984; Thomas, 1992).

REVIEW QUESTIONS

1. What is meant by the phrase "debatable question"?
2. Whenever your organization disagrees, what is the one truth it needs to keep in mind?
3. What role did the Caucasian Methodists play in the racial conflict in the United States?
4. Why did some Caucasians believe that social parity between Caucasians and African Americans was unachievable?
5. What is the difference between slavery and racial exclusion?
6. How will planting seeds now help an organization in the future?
7. How does equity theory relate to the Central Jurisdiction?
8. How does expectancy theory relate to the Central Jurisdiction?

9. Why did some Methodists believe that the Central Jurisdiction establishment was the right course of action for African Americans?
10. Why did African Americans protest the establishment of the African American jurisdiction?
11. Who was Bishop Thirkield, and what was his perspective on the slavery issue?
12. How does self-actualization relate to the Central Jurisdiction?
13. What are three lessons about organizational change that you learned in this chapter?
14. How should organizations handle internal forces?
15. What are some examples of external forces?
16. What are some ways that organizations can use external forces to can positively?

Chapter 3

RESISTANCE TO CHANGE IN THE METHODIST ORGANIZATION

LEARNING OBJECTIVES

- Contrast the two forms of resistance: symbolism and aggression.
- Discuss the various ways of resistance to change.
- Explain Bishop John Hamilton's ideological position on social equality.
- Explain why people resist change.

- Discuss the nine lessons about resistance that your business learned from the Methodist organization change process.
- Discuss the results of resistance.
- Explain what is needed to accomplish change.
- Define gatekeepers.
- Discuss three organizational change lessons that you learn in Chapter 3.

DURING THE 4TH CENTURY, PLATO POSTULATED, CHANGE WILL occur no matter who tries to discourage it. Change is inevitable, necessary, and expected. According to Sasikala and Anthonyraj (2015), "change is the only unchanging reality in the world" (p. 30). Kotter and Schlesinger (2008) suggested that many organizations have to make minor changes throughout the year and significant changes as often as every 4 to 5 years. This chapter explores the forms of resistance, the reasons people resist, and the nine lessons about resistance that we decipher from the defiance to change in the Methodist Church.

TWO FORMS OF RESISTANCE

Whenever organizations present change, there is a natural tendency for followers to resist because it involves moving from the familiar to the unfamiliar. It means giving up power. It also consists of reallocating resources. Giving up control and reallocating resources are why we saw Southern Caucasian Methodists establish a national front against desegregation (Davis, 2008; Huff, 2016).

Some of the national front resistances were in the form of symbolism; others were in aggression. For instance, Bishop William

Ragsdale Cannon was a symbol of resistance to desegregation in the Church. According to Davis (2008), Bishop Cannon, a Southern bishop who was "one of the strongest and most willful bishops in that church, emboldened the resistance to change among the MECS delegates. His presence seemed to steel the resolve of those who had offered the strongest resistance to compromise" (p. 107). He was a potent symbol of opposition.

After the *Brown v. Board of Education of Topeka* decision, southern Whites received the decision with hostile aggression. In six southern states, organizers instituted *segregation for forever* alliance in several conferences. One such collaboration was the Association of Methodist Ministers and Laymen to Preserve Established Racial Customs, which was a Klan-like organization to intimidate, persecute, and threaten ministers who advocated against segregation (Davis, 2008; Reiff, 2016; Richey et al., 2010).

If pastors trumpeted annihilating segregation, supported desegregating schools, and advocated improving better dialogue and collaboration between the races, some organizations and people threatened these pastors and their families. For some ministers who decided not to wait quietly for change, the Methodist Church removed them from congregations. No surge of support emerged from the superintendents and bishops to stop the harassment and cruelty.

Resistance to change can emerge from several factors, such as individuals, groups, and administrative levels (Sasikala & Anthonyraj, 2015). These individuals, groups, and organizational levels can represent their perspective by a stream of symbolism or blatant aggression and vitriol.

REASONS FOR RESISTANCE

Flamholtz and Randle (2008) asserted that several factors could cause an organization to resist or accept change, such as wanting to hold onto norms and values, being unwilling to accept innovation, and being unsuccessful in other change ventures. Harvey and Broyles (2010) listed several other reasons for resistance: hypercriticism, boredom, not being recognized, and insecurity. However, Klein's (2011) perspective on resistance to change differs in that resistance is generated because the evolution may not be beneficial. Resistance to change can also be crafty and vague.

Sometimes resistance to racial injustice in the Methodist Church was friendly, subtle, and collegial. These people showed support for African Americans' justice but fell short of recognizing that all people are created equal (Davis, 2008). MEC Bishop John Hamilton was one of these archetypes.

Hamilton stood out among the Joint Committee members for his position on full integration in the Church. Davis (2008) expressed that, although Hamilton was courageous, he had placed himself in a lonely position. Hamilton's stance on inclusivity was always his view. In Boston, which was his first appointment, he rallied people to raise money for Boston immigrants, worked with the Freedman's Aid Society, and advocated for African Americans' equity in the Church and community.

However, there was a line he would not cross. He believed in a class distinction between Caucasians, lower Caucasians, and African Americans. Moreover, Hamilton felt social equality among the other two classes—lower Caucasians and African Americans— threatened the Anglo–Saxon people in America (Davis, 2008).

MECS delegate, A. J. Lamar declared that Hamilton's racial ideology of resistance to change was not because of an unwillingness to accept innovation. Hamilton's racial position was not because integration was not suitable for Methodism. Instead, it was subtle racism and a sly and clever way of presenting his belief in a caste system.

NINE LESSONS FROM RESISTANCE TO CHANGE

There are nine lessons that we learn from the Methodist Church about resistance to change. **First**, resistance results from a loss of autonomy, making people feel they have lost control of their space. If people in your organization feel threatened or insecure, they will put their arms around the status quo to protect it. **Second**, resistance is also people's inability and unwillingness to adapt to change (Darling, 1993). **Third**, resistance to change could result from people's inability to see themselves organizing and employing actions to deliver the desired results. Sasikala and Anthonyraj (2015) explained that the perception of low self-efficacy is one of the influences that may cause resistance by intensifying the probability that the cognitive and emotional resistance engender resistance. In other words, resistance could be that the leaders see the task is too difficult to achieve.

The **fourth** lesson is that organizations that refuse to adapt and adjust to change could be creating a formula for their own demise (Gardner, 1995). Organizations that refuse to adapt set themselves up for extinction, which is why organizations need to understand that sometimes change is necessary.

Fifth, organizations also need to know that they must understand the psychological, emotional, and behavioral blocks they will encounter as they seek to change to accomplish the necessary changes. These factors have to be confronted and conquered if a change is to take place. **Sixth**, organizations must also understand that it is people who accomplish the change and not organizations.

Seventh, it does not matter how large an organization is or what kind of organization it is; there always must be a few people who are willing to step forward and take a risk. The direction and destiny of the organization will be controlled and maneuvered by these few people. **Eighth**, not all change is good from some people's perspectives, so these people serve as gatekeepers of resistance to any change that threatens the status quo. **Ninth**, great leaders expect change and know how to handle it. Regardless of what type of resistance people use, leaders need to understand that they must be ready for change and have processes to manage the change (Harvey & Broyles, 2010). Cameron and Green (2008) emphasized that understanding change is inevitable and knowing how to deal with it makes leaders and organizations effective.

REVIEW QUESTIONS

1. What do symbolism and aggression mean as they relate to change?
2. What are the reasons people object to change?
3. What are the various forms of resistance?
4. What is the role of a gatekeeper?
5. Discuss three organizational change lessons that you learned in Chapter 3.
6. What was Hamilton's perspective on social equity?
7. To change an organization, what do great leaders need to understand?
8. What are the nine lessons of resistance to change your organization learned from the Methodist organization change process?

Chapter 4
Achieving Successful Organizational Change

LEARNING OBJECTIVES

- Discuss what you or your organization learned about change as Paul traveled through Galatia and Corinth.
- Discuss the two types of change described by Mennella and Strayer.
- Explain the five models of change that your organization can use to transform its culture.
- Discuss the change model used during the Methodist Reformation to eliminate the Central Jurisdiction that can also help your organization.

- Explain some of the lessons your organization learned from the Methodist Reformation in each stage of the Lewin change model about the change process.
- Name some of the men and women who were change agents during the Methodist Reformation.
- Discuss the nine lessons learned from the Methodist Dilemma called the Central Jurisdiction that can help successfully transform any organization.

THIS CHAPTER EXAMINES THE LESSONS PAUL TAUGHT US ABOUT organizational change from his ministry in Galatia and Corinth. We explore the forms of change and the five models of change. We explore the Lewin (1951) change model and how the Methodist organization used it to transform the Methodist Church's culture and decipher the lessons your organization can use now. We also examine the lessons your organization should learn from the Methodist dilemma that will help your business successfully change itself for the better.

ORGANIZATIONAL LESSONS LEARNED FROM THE METHODIST DILEMMA

The Methodist dilemma called the Central Jurisdiction teaches us that to successfully transform your organization, it must (a) establish a change team; (b) understand how plans work; (c) learn and choose a model of change; (d) select change agents with courage; (e) set goals and priorities for the change team; (f) challenge the organizational culture, vision, and goals; (g) choose transformational leadership to articulate the vision; (h) overcome resistance to change; and (i) connect the change to the broader vision.

Establish a Change Team

The organizational change that percolated in the Methodist Church to eliminate the Central Jurisdiction teaches us that change involves establishing a change team focused primarily on what is necessary for the organization to change. American author and political activist Helen Keller (n.d.) declared, "The only thing worse than being blind is having sight but no vision" (para. 19). Once you have chosen your change team, the vision is the power that will shape your organization's way forward. It is a tool your organization can use to help your company break out of its current comfort zone and continually see its better self.

Paul's vision for the churches at Galatia and Corinth served as his strategy and destination. He said although they were different, they were one in the Body of Christ. In the Body of Christ, "there is no longer Jew or Greek, there is no longer slave or free, there is no longer male and female; for all of you are one in Christ Jesus" (Gal. 3:28; New Revised Standard Version). Paul established a team in both churches, and he conveyed to those teams the message that they should deliver to the masses. The Methodist Church's Central Jurisdiction also had a team. That group was chasing after a vision.

The organizational change lesson. The lesson that can be learned from this is that, based on the organizational change in the Methodist Church, in the change management process, your organization needs to establish a change team with a focus on what is necessary for the change. Without a clear picture of your between goals and end goals and a designated unit to coalesce people around that clear picture, your organization will perish.

The change team members will need to be change agents who understand the end and keep the end in mind. They will create a realistic plan. They will also communicate openly and clearly, identify major players, and delegate tasks. The team will also set smart, manageable, attainable, and realistic goals; supervise expectations; and make sure people follow through.

Understand How Change Plans Work

According to Mennella, Strayer, and Pravikoff (2016), there are two types of change: drift and planned. The drift plan is also called an emergent plan. Drift planning is accidental, with no strategy. Organizations do not make any decision about the process that they will use to birth change.

The leaders are attempting to avoid taking responsibility for the conclusions or failed outcomes. They could be trying to avoid an argument about the change. Moreover, they could be seeking to please everyone who is a part of the change process or the organization itself, or the leaders are trying to avoid their doubts or insecurities.

Drifting into a plan of action usually leaves organizations not bringing to maturity their goals. It can also cause organizations to lose their strategic momentum. Of course, drifting into an idea is not recommended.

Planned change is strategic. It involves either preparing part of the organization or the entire organization for new ideas, concepts, programs, thinking, and structures. These new ideas or designs could be in organizational culture, internal or external processes, or compensation. Planned change is also well thought out and involves institutions putting the right people in place to get the job done and having a change model. Collins (2001) asserted, in his book *Good to Great*, to get the right team so that an organization can obtain its goals, the business must get the right people on the bus and get those people in the right seats and get the wrong people off the bus.

Either of these plans—emergent or planned—alone is not recommended. However, a combination of the two gives the organization and change agents the ability to develop concrete proposals and allow ideas to emerge on the journey of transformation.

Most organizations' environments are not stable and predictable. Many organizations have a great start but then, over time, lose their influence. Often, organizations do have strategic plans, but unforeseen consequences emerge because their members sometimes respond differently than the organization had predicted. Using a combination of planned change and emergent change will help your organizations deal with dynamic environments.

The organizational change lesson. One organizational change lesson that can be gleaned from this is one of the outcomes we learn from trampling underfoot the all-Black area of the Church is that planned change and emergent change are not independent of each other. They are not in conflict. For your business to view these two plans as separate actually confines them.

To change the Methodist structure to deal with the deep-seated problem of race, the Methodist Church planned several proposals and implemented those irons in the fire, such as the Committee of Five. Suppose the all-Black area had not put in place, from the beginning, the Committee of Five. In that case, the goals of putting six feet under all forms of discrimination in the Church, which went beyond just abolishing the Central Jurisdiction, may not have been an objective of the Methodist denomination.

From this planned group came concrete plans to "(1) realign the wide-ranging annual conferences of the Central Jurisdiction and (2) transfer entire annual conferences from the Central Jurisdiction to regional jurisdictions" (Thomas, 1992, p. 121). This planned group— the Committee of Five—helped jettison the arduous idea of transferring local churches. They provided a better course of action to help the annual conferences merge more smoothly (and without a hitch) regional conference. However, several plans to change the Methodist structure to root out the all-Black jurisdiction, which was unplanned, emerged along the way. These were plans that naturally and unpredictably came to fruition as the African American conference implemented the change process. To depend totally on random change would have made the Central Jurisdiction change process chaotic, messy, and unbearable.

On the other hand, to depend totally on planned change would have made the organizational change agents inflexible, keeping the change agents from devising plans that made the evolution smoother, more comfortable, and manageable.

The organizational change lesson. Another organizational change lesson is this: first, your organization needs to combine both planned and emergent organizational change methods. Combining planned and emergent approaches will help your leaders understand how to process change adequately (Tarandach & Bartunek, 2009). Merging planned and emergent change is similar to what Bennis (2009) calls whole-brain thinking. Although the left brain dominates many human beings, people are both left brain and right brain thinkers. The brain's left side enables us to be logical, precise, technical, controlled, conservative, and administrative. The brain's right side empowers us to be more intuitive, flexible, synthesizing, and artistic.

Bennis gives a specific example of how the whole brain approach works: We use our brains' left side to make habits. And we use the right side to unmake those habits. Study after study shows that whole-brain thinking—planned and emergent change combined—helps organizations get better results.

Second, a "one or the other" understanding of planned growth and emergent change keeps the plans from strengthening each other. They depend on each other. They are partners that will work together to influence your organization profoundly. For your business to view these two plans as separate will keep your organization from adequately using the strategies to help you create a better way forward.

Third, a "one or the other" understanding of planned change and emergent change prevents the plans from generating new ideas that will enhance your organization's change process.

Fourth, your organization will devise its organizational strategies at the beginning of your change process. Your blueprint will also emerge as you journey through the process. From the very beginning of your change method, your organization will set goals. As you discuss your goals and seek to execute them, new ideas will surface, causing your organization to always be in motion and reinventing your organizational plan.

Learn Change Models and Choose One

There are several models of change. Sometimes organizations may realize that they are using one or more of these models, and sometimes they will not. Let me highlight five of them. Afterward, I underscore the one closely resembling the Central Jurisdiction change agents model to transform the Methodist Church structure.

Kubler-Ross change curve (or the change curve model). Elizabeth Kubler-Ross developed the change curve model in the 1960s. This model consists of five stages: denial, anger, bargaining, depression, and acceptance (Kubler-Ross & Kessler, 2014; Santrock, 2007).

1. Denial is the first stage. In this stage, there is an initial shock, brief lethargy, and decreased productivity. People who are usually shocked seek more assistance and directions. People are typically shocked because some entities or people kept them in the dark about the situation, or they don't know what will happen next, or they fear incompetence. This shock leads to denial. There is a feeling that nothing needs to change. Everything is all right or will be all right.
2. Anger is the second stage. During this process, you see people in the organization looking for a scapegoat, someone to blame, so that the denial can continue.
3. Bargaining is the third stage. After the phase of anger subsides, people may start to contemplate how to put on ice the unavoidable.
4. Depression is the fourth stage. Once the blame and anger go under the surface, depression begins to set in because the organization's members realize that change is real.

During this stage, effectiveness and proficiency have hit rock bottom.
5. Acceptance is the fifth stage. As organization members move through the anger and depression stage, optimism and enthusiasm begin to surface. Members start to see the change as opportunities for new ideas, new leadership, and new productivity.

Lewin's change plan model. In the 1940s, Kurt Lewin (1951) created the change plan model, which has three stages: unfreeze, change, and refreeze.

1. In the unfreezing stage, the leaders prepare the organization with a compelling message for why change is essential. The persuasive report involves explaining why the things that helped the organization get to its present point in history are not enough to take it into the future. Leadership must convince the organization's members why the status quo of beliefs, values, *modus operandi*, and customs cannot hold out and put up a fight against the new emerging trends.
2. In the change stage, members begin to brainstorm to find new, fresh, and forward-looking ways to go in a different direction. Going another direction will be a slow process because members will have to take on new responsibilities and duties. Immediate resolutions probably will not be seen, and some chaos may occur. But members must see this change process as an investment, which will produce recommendations that will improve the organization.

3. In the refreeze stage, which is the last stage of Lewin's change process, the organization takes steps to make the changes permanent. The changes become a part of the organization's daily operating system. It also means incorporating and institutionalizing the changes to be part of the regular decision-making pattern, accountability, and the implementation process.

The refreeze stage does not mean that the organization will not make more changes. Once the organization plugs in the new policies and procedures that give organizational members stability and confidence, better ways of doing things will continue to emerge because of the changes or the new process.

Kotter's theory. Kotter (1990) developed an eight-stage process for change.

1. Create a sense of urgency. Get as many people as you can to feel that change is imperative. Honest dialogue needs to discuss why the organization is not as effective as possible and what will continue to happen to the organization if new ways of doing things are not discovered and implemented.
2. Assemble a guiding coalition. To envision change, formulate, and implement it, you need leaders who are change agents. You have to form a team of these change agent leaders from various levels and multiple departments or areas of the organization that have influence. This team will continue to articulate the change message so that the momentum and energy for change continues.

Achieving successful organizational change

3. Outline a calculated plan (vision) and initiatives. All organizations plan to accomplish goals, but to succeed, organizations need to create a clear vision, which means putting in writing what the organization is trying to achieve. It makes changes more tangible and generates support to execute the idea. It helps organizational leaders and members accept directives and understand that specific steps or tasks are necessary.
4. Recruit helpers to convey the calculated plan. There needs to be a designated team of people who continue to talk about the vision in various ways and forums. There will be many voices competing for the organizational members' attention. Organizations need to appoint designated people to communicate the plan every chance they get and listen to others' opinions and worries for organizations to win this battle. Organizations must obtain buy-in from most of the organizational members.
5. Get rid of the barriers. When you reach this stage of the process, you will have talked about your vision differently to various people in your organization. Although your vision may be getting across to organizational members, barriers make the vision for change more difficult. Always find ways to remove these barriers. Eliminating barriers can galvanize and energize corporate members. You will need to implement your new ideas for growth and effectiveness.
6. Generate wins as you journey toward the ultimate vision. Make sure you have little wins and celebrate them. The small successes will fire up the members of your team. These wins will also motivate them to continue to want to

change because they see the results. Making it a priority to plan wins early in the change process will encourage those who have bought into the new way of doing things and hamper critics and naysayers.
7. Sustain the changes by building on them. Don't make the mistake that many leaders and organizations do—declaring victory too soon. As you have little wins, you will discover what you do best. Keep doing better what you do best. Keep improving the process. Continue to look at what worked and what failed and adjust what did not work, so it works better the next time.
8. Fasten the adjustments to the organizational culture. The final stage of Kotter's change process involves making sure the changes stick to the organization's ribs. You want to make sure the changes are not a fad but a part of who you are. Organizations need to ensure that corporate members see the changes in every organization's area using bulletin boards, slogans, newsletters, and rewards.

ADKAR Model. Jeff Hiatt (2006) created a change process using the acronym ADKAR, which stands for *awareness, desire, knowledge, ability*, and *reinforcement*.
1. **Awareness** that a change is needed to make the organization as effective as it can be
2. **Desire** to be involved in the change process and to support whatever changes are required
3. **Knowledge** about the process that it takes to facilitate change
4. **Ability** to use the skills and behaviors necessary to facilitate change

5. **Reinforcement** to maintain the change

The ADKAR model is a practical means for planning change management activities, preparing leaders for making changes, and supporting organizational members throughout the entire change process. Hiatt believed the five outcomes, ADKAR, must be achieved in sequential order to have lasting change. When organizations have implemented changes that failed, Hiatt thought it was because they have not realized one or more outcomes.

The Satir change management model. Virginia Satir (1991) developed the Satir change management model. Satir designed it to help people and organizations deal with significant and anticipated change. In this change model, there are five stages.
1. Late status quo: This stage is the unchanged state of affairs. Things are running as they usually do. A problem occurs that causes the whole team to adjust, which leads to dysfunctionalism, such as placing the blame, appeasing, resentment, and absenteeism.
2. Resistance: Organizations enter this stage because the dysfunctionalism disturbs the late status quo. For the organization to address the dysfunctionalism, the organization introduces a new way of operating, which is called a foreign element. It is unfamiliar because it is not a part of the present *modus operandi*. Those who are used to the structure, as it is, seek to block the new way of doing things (foreign element) by denying that there is a problem, circumventing the matter, or blaming others for causing the dysfunctionalism.

3. Chaos: The new way of doing things spins the organization into a stage of turmoil where people feel worried, perplexed, afraid, unhappy, uncomfortable, and desperate. Business as usual is disappearing or on the verge of extinction. Members of the organization try to go back to the project they are familiar with using hammers and nails. But they quickly discover that this does not alleviate the distress because the simple project requires them to design the project first and then email it to the department head. Members are still confused and uncomfortable. This stage is not a good feeling but can lead to creativity.
4. Integration: In this stage, organizational members consider how they can implement this new operating way. They also contemplate how they can use it and how it can improve their work. Members build new relationships, form new teams, and develop new partnerships.
5. New status quo: In this stage, the new way of doing things has become a part of the organizational culture. The new way of operating creates new ideas, new energy, new relationships, and improved productivity. Members master new skills.

These are just a few of the types of planned change models that your organization can use to transform your organizational cultures.

THE METHODIST ORGANIZATIONAL CHANGE METHOD

It seems, although the Methodist change agents may not have known it during the Methodist Reformation, Lewin's (1951) model was used to change the Methodist organizational culture. During the first stage of the Methodist Reformation, the **unfreezing phase**, the Central Jurisdiction had to convince the General Conference to accept its changes. The church's all-African American branch proceeded by developing a compelling message that challenged the Methodist Church's beliefs, values, and attitudes. The African American jurisdiction challenged the existing foundation of Methodism, which stated that we are all God's children. The challenge was this: If we are all God's children, then none of us should in any way be marginalized, demeaned, or diminished.

If this is the case, then the separate but equal practice in the Methodist denomination was unacceptable for the Church of Jesus Christ. Change agents from the Central Jurisdiction, such as Bishop Bowen, conveyed that African Americans are not second-class citizens in the Church. The apartheid system in the Methodist organization that separated its members based on race was heresy. Separate but equal in the Church was not American Christian patriotism. It was sacrilege and harmful to the Methodist Church's soul.

This first stage was the most difficult, stressful, and traumatic. When you seek to challenge the status quo, people fear losing control, past resentments, and status loss. Therefore, during this first stage, strong emotions were evoked—those who wanted it and those who did not.

Joseph Lowery reminded the Church that African Americans were black because God made them black. Black people's color should not keep them from being fully included in the Church. On the other side of the coin were strong emotions from such men as John Moore, who believed that mixed-race denominations would hinder African American pastors' and churches' progress. Although these convictions evoked strong emotions because the Central Jurisdiction force the Methodist Church to reexamine its existing foundation, the process was manageable.

Since the Methodist Reformation was partly a planned change process, the Methodist Church could control the crisis and heart-wrenching passions. That is one reason your establishment needs to connect intentional change and emergent change; it helps your organization be flexible enough to reexamine itself voluntarily. Socrates said, "The unexamined life is not worth living" (Quote Analysis: The Unexamined Life, n.d.). Bennis (2009) told us that people or institutions cannot move forward unless they examine their past.

> The unexamined life is impossible to live successfully. Like oarsmen, we generally move forward while looking backward but not until we truly see the past—and understand it—can we successfully navigate the future (p. 64).

Your organization's successful future depends on learning from the past. It depends on understanding what past and present mistakes not to make in the future.

Also, by joining planned change and emergent change, your organization will be better positioned to manage the various crises that will undoubtedly emerge. On the contrary, if your organization's plans are rigid, then your leadership team will be highly unlikely to make wise, appropriate, and impromptu decisions as situations materialize.

After the challenge of the status quo in the first stage, which created uncertainty and strong emotions, the people called Methodist began to discuss ways to extinguish the all-African American conference (**change stage**). In this stage, the Church addressed doubts and fears. The Church also discussed new ways of being the Church after liquidating the racial jurisdictional structure and merger. The people on the opposite end of the ocean were no longer ships passing in the night. The members' feelings started to work together to lead, mold, and brand the Methodist denomination's new organizational culture.

The process from **unfreeze to change** was tedious and did not happen overnight. It took constant work and maneuvering to get buy-in for the new direction, get people to change, and get them to participate in the change. It took convincing people to understand that the new path would benefit all involved and help the Methodist Church be who it claimed to be.

The organizational change lesson. One organizational change lesson that can be learned from the Methodist Reformation is that not everyone will agree with the new direction and agree to participate in the new process. Your organization should expect these disagreements in any organizational change. Some will jump ship because the evolution is too much. Nevertheless, your business needs to take all measures to get as many as possible to buy into the dream.

Your organization's objective should be to let deep ambition and love for the organization propel you and not let the naysayers keep the ship from sailing forward. And remember that the process from unfreeze to change is not immediate. The stern resisters will spurn and reject change, so your organization must keep hope alive as you adventurously journey toward more prosperous days by encouraging your members. Encouraging your people will help them stay resilient.

The Methodist Reformation, merging the Methodist Church and the Central Jurisdiction, took time and communication. Whatever organization you are trying to change, remember that it is a slow process, and your organization will need to have plenty of conversation. People tend to drift toward what they are familiar with, even if that usual place is harmful, destructive, or toxic. People are creatures of habit, and it takes time and encouragement to break habits.

The last stage of the Methodist Reformation was to **refreeze**. During the discussions, steps were being put in place to get rid of the Black jurisdiction, and agreements were being solidified by putting them in writing in the United Methodist Discipline, the document that contains the Church's polity.

The organizational change lesson. Another organizational change lesson to learn is it is prudent to understand that your organization can implement change, but things can revert to the old ways if your business does not cement new beliefs, values, and behaviors into the organizational culture.

The new standards and norms must become the new order of the day and must enlarge the future. When you cement in writing, the changes, policies, and procedures do not mean your organization will not need to make further changes later. It is highly likely that the new changes will create new teams and relationships that will birth new ideas of how your corporation can work more effectively. By making the new standards the new norm, your business will be helping your members grow into and with the new way. It will inject in them a shared sense of direction and purpose.

Although the Methodist organization may not have known the change model it was using, it would be beneficial to your organization to be proactive, learn a model, and implement the change your organization wants. It will help your business manage its change and learn to adjust to change when necessary. It will also help your organization keep focused on what it is trying to do at every step of the change process. For instance, in the Lewin (1951) model of change, your organization's first step would be to explain why change is needed.

In the first step, you would also include teaching your organizational members the benefits of changing. The next step is to make changes. Lastly, after your corporate members present, accept, and adopt the changes, your organization would put those policies in place to ensure your company routinely uses them. Every change model presents some course of action. Your organization will need to review and study the change process models present in this chapter. Then you will need to decide what model best fits the decisions your organization needs to make. Then choose and put into practice that model.

Choose Change Agents With Courage

The Methodist Reformation teaches us that there is more to be considered when trying to change an organization, whether it is a church, a denomination, a country, or a business. Your organization needs to learn the models of change and choose one to help with implementing the organizational change, and your business needs to understand this—it is challenging to produce change without courage and change agents (Amos & Klimoski, 2014).

In Paul's day, he had the courage and was the change agent in the Galatian and Corinthian churches. Courage in the Methodist Church came from organizations, such as the Methodist Women and the Committee of Five. Courage also came from individuals, such as James Farmer, George Houser, Charles C. Parlin, Dorothy Rogers Tilly, Dr. James Thomas, Dr. Davage, Dr. James T. Brawley, and Mary McLeod Bethune. With great emphasis, these individuals jumped all over delegates, asking them to reject the 1935 Plan of Union. They were the change agents in the Methodist Church. Through calm demeanor, constancy, and strength like steel, Paul, in his situations, and James Farmer, George Houser, Dr. Thomas, Dr. Matthew Davage, Dr. Brawley, and others in their circumstances took courage into both hands and challenged and changed their respective organizational systems.

The organizational change lesson. The lesson here is your organization will need to choose lionhearted leaders. There will be times that your leaders will have to take bold steps and make unpopular decisions. Influential leaders have several skills that make them useful, but one of the necessary skills is bravery. Walt Disney (Mickey Blog, 2018), a former CEO of Walt Disney World, said, "Courage is the main quality of leadership; in my opinion, no matter where it is exercised. Usually, it implies some risk—especially in new undertakings" (para. 11).

Franklin D. Roosevelt (n.d.) stated, "Courage is not the absence of fear, but rather the assessment that something else is more important than fear" (para. 1). Nelson Mandela (n.d.) said, "I learned that courage was not the absence of fear, but the triumph over it" (section 1). To change your organization so that it is more productive, you will need leaders who do not always play it safe. Your organization will never accomplish its change and new dreams without daring leaders who are willing to take risks.

Set Goals and Priorities for the Change Team

The process of dismantling the Black jurisdiction also teaches us that to have a significant organizational change process, organizations need to establish goals and priorities for the team. Your organization's goals will help to determine the change team's primary concerns. Therefore, your corporation's goals will drive the team's priorities. Your goals will also help the team have a long-term focus and help keep the team from drifting aimlessly from one issue to another. To make sure your change team's reason for existing stays front and center, frequently answer these questions along your change journey.

- What are the advantages and disadvantages of changing the organization?
- What groundwork has your institution laid for organizational change?

- What is your team doing to build consensus along the way?
- What is your team doing to remain transparent?
- What is the positive impact on both leaders and followers?
- What is your establishment doing to keep the communications aligned with the changes?
- Can you sketch the big picture?
- What does the big picture look like?

Challenge the Organizational Culture, Vision, and Goals

Order with the end in mind. The organizational change that transpired in the Methodist Church to eliminate the Central Jurisdiction teaches us *change involves challenging the corporate culture, vision, and goals*. Organizations, leaders, and scholars have defined culture in a variety of ways. Coeling and Simms (1993) described culture as "values developed by a group in order to survive their tasks, a set of beliefs shared by the group, expected behaviours, a set of solutions for problems they face in common" (p. 3). Schein (1996) defined culture as "set of basic tacit assumptions about how the world is and ought to be that a group of people share and that determines their perceptions, thoughts, feelings, and, to some degree, their overt behavior" (p. 11).

The organizational change lesson is, to challenge your organization's culture, vision, and goals, your leadership along with its members needs to have a clear view of the organization's desired direction and destination. Stephen Covey called it thinking with the end in mind. What does your organization value? What do you want members, employees, and partners to say about you? How do you want to be remembered? If your organization does not presently look like you want it to be, use one of the change models discussed in this chapter to determine what needs to be changed and change it.

Prepare for the change

In 1956, when so many had advocated that it was time to change the Methodist Church's racial culture, Bishop James Thomas (1992) said, "The dilemma at that point was facing the reluctance to abolish the Central Jurisdiction by many within The Methodist Church" (p. 87). Bishop Thomas was saying that it was time to change. The only question left to answer was this: is the Church committed to the change? Dr. Thomas felt to help the Church answer this question, leaders of the Church had to continue to share the vision of an inclusive church.

The organizational change lesson is, to prepare your organization for a change, you will have to continue to share the vision of a new and improved organization. Your members need to know more than just that you will be improving your company; they also need to understand why the improvements are essential. You will have to communicate this vision frequently in meetings, emails, text, newsletters, posters, etc.

Deal with the fears

Caucasians were fearful that African Americans would be unforgiving for all the ill treatment received during segregation.

Robert Elijah Jones argued that African Americans were naturally humble and forgiving people (Davis, 2008). He hoped that the demonstration of thousands of African American men who volunteered for the United States Armed Forces, notwithstanding Jim Crow laws, would convey to White Americans that Whites did not need to fear African American backlash.

The organizational change lesson is that your organization will need to deal with your corporate members' fears. The fears of change will be a real emotion you cannot ignore. These anxieties will inhibit your members from embracing the new and throwing out the old. To deal with these fears, you will have to sell the idea that the future will be better than the present. Day after day and week after week, you will have to publicize that shredding the old baggage is more beneficial than being a prisoner of the past. Promoting your organization's new way of life means you will need to communicate in as many ways as possible about the coming changes' positive benefits.

Deal with what is and what is not

For proponents of integration, during the steps to uproot the Central Jurisdiction, they had to describe, articulate, and continuously explain what full and extensive integration in the Methodist Church looked like for African Americans. Blacks made it plain that comprehensive integration (and this was made evident) was not merely accommodating African Americans in a racially segregated jurisdiction. They did not want the Methodist Church to appease them. Appeasement would not allow them to utilize their God-given gifts to their full potential. African Americans did not want to latch on to full membership and lose the most important things they could bring to the table to make the Church better—their gifts and talents.

The organizational change lesson is, as you change your organization, you have to define what that change is and what it is not. You have to describe in writing the change that should be acquired by the end of the change process.

You also must lay on the table, repeatedly, the nonnegotiable items. In other words, your organization must make clear those things that are not up for debate. There are some things your company does well. There is a proverb that says, "Don't throw the baby out with the bathwater." In other words, do not get rid of something that you do well, along with something undesirable. Even if you lose some of the fights, as did those supporting integration and those who wanted to abolish the all-African American Region, at least the deal breakers will be clear. These nonnegotiable factors will be there to guide you through difficult times and help you identify what you do well. Then, along with the necessary changes, you can do better what you do best.

Choose Transformational Leadership to Articulate the Vision

The organizational change that transpired in the Methodist Church to eliminate the Central Jurisdiction teaches us *change involves transformational leadership*. Transformational leadership was one of the keys to successful organizational change in the Methodist Church. What is transformational leadership? Bass and Riggio posited (2006) that transformational leaders engage and inspire others to go beyond the call of duty to achieve extraordinary outcomes.

Going beyond the call of duty is what Paul did; as a transformational leader, he helped the churches attain exceptional results. He inspired the churches at Galatia and Corinth to look beyond what made them different.

> The human body has many parts, but the many parts make up one whole body. So, it is with the body of Christ. Some of us are Jews, some are Gentiles, some are slaves, and some are free. But we have all been baptized into one body by one Spirit, and we all share the same Spirit.
>
> Yes, the body has many different parts, not just one part. If the foot says, "I am not a part of the body because I am not a hand," that does not make it any less a part of the body. And if the ear says, "I am not part of the body because I am not an eye," would that make it any less a part of the body? If the whole body were an eye, how would you hear? Or if your whole body were an ear, how would you smell anything?
>
> But our bodies have many parts, and God has put each part just where he wants it. How strange a body would be if it had only one part! Yes, there are many parts, but only one body. The eye can never say to the hand, "I don't need you." The head can't say to the feet, "I

don't need you." (1 Corinthians 12:12-21, New Living Translation)

Those followers of Christ who possessed stunning gifts had no use for those who had lesser skills than they had. Paul taught that every member of the Body of Christ is an integral part of the church's life, health, and maturity. No Jesus follower can say to another, "I don't need you in my life." We cannot see those parts of our body with our physical eye because they are external organs, such as the brain, heart, lungs, and kidneys; however, they are essential in keeping human beings alive. Or they can cause much trouble to our health if they do not function properly. Therefore, Paul said that there should be no division (splits) in the Body. Why? Because all of Jesus' followers share the same life with the Spirit. Paul explained,

> In fact, some parts of the body that seem weakest and least important are actually the most necessary. And the parts we regard as less honorable are those we clothe with the greatest care. So, we carefully protect those parts that should not be seen, while the more honorable parts do not require this special care. So God has put the body together such that extra honor and care are given to those parts that have less dignity. This makes for harmony among the members, so that all the members care for each other. If one part suffers, all the parts suffer with it, and if one part is honored, all the parts are glad.
>
> All of you together are Christ's body, and each of you is a part of it. (1 Cor. 12:12-27, New Living Translation)

Paul, a transformational leader in his day, said to the church to look at what each part of the Body had to offer to the Body of Christ's functioning and effectiveness. To exclude any of these gifts, for whatever reason, would diminish the Body, not enhance it. In the 1952 Episcopal Address, we see this inspirational and transformational leadership that was needed come from Bishop Paul Kern:

> To discriminate against a person solely upon the basis of his race is both unfair, and unchristian [sic]. Every child of God is entitled to that place in society that he has won by his industry, his integrity, and his character. To deny him that position of honor because of the accident of his birth is neither honest democracy nor good religion. ("General Conference of 1952," 1952, p. 64)

Transformational leadership clearly explains the issues and urges followers to accept change. Transformational leaders also motivate their followers to do better. While transformational leaders motivate others to achieve extraordinary outcomes, they seek to help followers develop their own gifts and leadership skills. Bass and Bass (2008) posited that transformational leaders (a) enable followers to become leaders themselves and (b) "convert self-interest into collective concerns" (p. 19). Burns (1978) made it clear that these types of leaders "engage followers, not merely activate them, to commingle needs and aspirations and goals in a common enterprise" (p. 461). Northouse (2012) defined these leaders as leaders concerned with their followers' emotions, principles, morals, goals, objectives, needs, and well-being.

The organizational change that transpired in the Methodist Church to eliminate the Central Jurisdiction teaches us that for organizational change to occur, the leadership must be transformational by articulating the vision and causing others to better themselves. Transformational leaders stretch their followers' dreams and hopes. They are men and women who can be boundless wellsprings of inspiration. Transformational leadership encompasses many aspects of life. However, it has at least one thing in common with the democratic, strategic, team, and cross-cultural leadership styles; a person or group can describe a better future and better people and arouse others to work toward this end (Mennella et al., 2016).

When the Joint Committee presented its unification plan, which called for several Caucasian regional jurisdictions and one African American jurisdiction, the Methodist women's transformational leadership condemned the plan (Davis, 2008). The Southern women, who had already been laboring through the Commission on Interracial Cooperation for improved relationships between Caucasians and African Americans, also challenged the plan. Both women's organizations of the MEC and MECS continued to work steadily and tirelessly against unimaginable racial inequality in secular and sacred institutions.

James T. Brawley, a thoughtful and transformational leader in his own right, continued through the jurisdictional structure's life to describe the vision. He conveyed that the Methodist Church's goal should be to terminate an unhealthy church structure and create an energetic body that radiated health. He expressed that the goal should also be to improve African Americans' status in the Methodist Church by putting to death the racial structure and creating a genuinely united Church that included all Methodist members (Brawley, 1967).

Bishop Loder was another thoughtful and transformational leader who described the vision—what the Methodist Church should be. In 1967, Bishop Loder, one of the Church's White bishops, came to the Central Jurisdiction in place of Bishop Donald Tippet, who could not attend. Loder declared that the Methodist Church had concluded it was time to dismantle a national symbol in our Church that excluded another race of people (Thomas, 1992). He said that this was not all that needed to be done to right this wrong, but it was a sizeable step in the right direction. Moreover, Bishop Loder expounded that since we are followers of the Lord, it was the right thing to do to dismantle committees, boards, annual conferences, and local churches that degrade people and keep them from fully participating in the Methodist denomination.

Transformational leadership members articulate a vision that convincingly inspires followers. The vision becomes a magnetic force drawing others to it. Transformational leaders also disseminate and broadcast a vision that improves organizational citizenship. They ask people to do more than the organization asks them to do and speak up for issues they otherwise would not. Transformational leaders, such as Mary McLeod Bethune, Hester Williams, Bishop Elijah Jones, Thelma Stevens, Bishop Willis J. King, Bishop James Thomas, Dr. James P. Brawley, Dr. W. Astor Kirk, Bishop Loder, and others articulated a vision that inspired people to help mold the Methodist Church into the spiritually, relationally, and psychologically healthy and saving instrument that God wanted it to be.

The organizational change lesson. The lesson here is, you will need transformational leaders who are visionaries. In other words, for changes to take place, internal forces (and external influencers) must lay out a roadmap that points to a brighter tomorrow. You need leaders who galvanize and stir your people to organize and create change that will help mature and mold your organization's future achievements. The bottom line is you need principal architects, general contractors, and brick masons to tear down the old way and build the new, and you must surround your organization with leaders who are like athletic coaches who are positive and can push your organization toward greatness.

Overcome Resistance to Change

To overcome resistance to change and implement change successfully, leaders possessing high organizational commitment are prerequisites (Visagie & Steyn, 2011). Change agents must be committed to the organization whenever the company engages in change because, if so, many benefits will result. According to Visagie and Steyn (2011), some of those benefits are that people who have high organizational commitment will extend their energy to ensure the changes are successfully implemented, work beyond the call of duty, and stand as ambassadors for the changes.

High organizational commitment and elevated self-efficacy are also needed to overcome resistance to change and implement change successfully. Bandura (1997) defined self-efficacy as people's belief that they can succeed in particular conditions or accomplish tasks. People with high self-efficacy in their abilities to achieve goals approach challenges as obstacles to overcome. They do not view challenges as dangers or risks or perils.

People with high self-efficacy also establish challenging goals and do all within their power to stay committed to those goals. These types of people do whatever is necessary to amplify and maintain their endeavors in the face of failure. So, to succeed in your organizational change process, you will need to identify leaders who have high organizational commitment and strong self-efficacy. One of the tools you can use to measure organizational commitments is Mowday et al.'s (1979) nine-item scale. To measure self-efficacy, you can use Morrison and Phelps' (1999) 10-item taking charge scale.

Organizations empowering their entities by creating flexibility in the organization and **establishing autonomy to communicate with the appropriate messages** whenever necessary is key to overcoming resistance. Without flexibility, your organization will be rigid, thereby setting itself up for failure. According to Bass and Bass (2008), your organization needs to empower your leaders and members. How? Your establishment will need to express that the business always needs to balance adaptation, stability, denial, and reality acceptance. "For example, 'we're not number one yet, but we will be.' The old forms can be abandoned, and the new can be better" (Bass & Bass, 2008, p. 36). Flexibility will unchain your company and permit it to adapt more effectively to unstable environments.

The Methodist Church demonstrated its commitment to change, overcoming resistance to change, implementing change, and becoming a better church than it was at the time by establishing several committees to study the racial dilemma. One of the last study committees (discussed earlier in this book) formed before the Methodist Church removed the Black jurisdiction was the Committee of Five (Thomas, 1992).

The members had to "analyze the proposals, recommendations, and actions of the Commission on Interjurisdictional Relations as they relate to the Central Jurisdiction" (Thomas, 1992, p. 166). They had to have face-to-face meetings with various people and annual conferences. They had to give progress reports, continuously negotiate, demonstrate flexibility, believe they could achieve their desired outcomes, and build consensus. They also had to respond effectively to letters from internal forces against and for the all-African American conference's extinction. They restated and enforced the desired outcomes of ridding the Methodist Church of the Central Jurisdiction and injustice and why it was necessary.

What is also vital for your organization to overcome resistance so that your business can implement change is to have teams or committees committed to the dream. Having people who can communicate the vision is also crucial. If your company's mental picture is blurred to how your organization will function after 2 to 3 years, your vision will not motivate people to give their best. When people do not understand the idea, they resist. Your organization's commitment to the dream and the ability to communicate that vision effectively will empower your organization and enhance the probability of your success (Yukl, 2002, p. 290).

Leadership Qualities to Overcome Resisters

According to Bishop Thomas, the committee consisted of people who had specific qualities. **First**, they had the technical, human, and conceptual skills to accomplish their mandate. **Second**, they were willing to step forward and take a risk. **Third**, they were committed to the process of change, which means they were ready to extend their energy to ensure the changes were successfully implemented, work beyond the call of duty, and stand as ambassadors for the changes (Visagie & Steyn, 2011). **Fourth**, they believed the Committee of Five could achieve the objectives.

Bishop Thomas stated that the Methodist Church saddled the Committee of Five with challenging responsibilities. After the Committee of Five studied the past study committee's work, conversed with annual conference members, responded to letters, and analyzed reports and proposals, they decided they would add two things to their responsibilities. These two goals were objectives the other committees had been unable to accomplish: (a) develop an all-inclusive, wide-ranging, and progressive strategy so that the Church could use Amendment IX to transfer all-African American annual conferences and (b) build trust to achieve consensus within the Central Jurisdiction (Thomas, 1992). The Committee decided that trust and consensus were necessary so that the committee's work would be honored, confirmed, and accepted. Also, the Committee of Five wanted the Methodist Church to say that the African American jurisdiction played a significant role in the ejection of the Central Jurisdiction and the Methodist Church's uniting.

The organizational change lesson. The lesson here is this: the Central Jurisdiction teaches us that change agent's success or failure of overcoming resistance to change and organizational transformation is closely related to the leader's (change agent's) level of organizational commitment; level of self-efficacy; balance, meaning flexibility; and autonomy to communicate. These four traits must be kept in mind when you choose your change agents. Why?

First of all, your change agents who possess these four traits, as demonstrated by the Committee of Five, will meaningfully contribute to your organization's goals and help your change agents go beyond the call of duty. **Second**, your change agents will be highly unlikely to quit. **Third**, your organization will need sacrifices. Your change agents will be more apt to make the required sacrifices. **Fourth**, your change agents will be more prone to participate fully in the change process. **Fifth**, they will engage in positive behaviors that help sustain, support, and strengthen your business's change initiatives (Bouckenooghe, Schwarz, & Minbashian, 2015).

Connect the Change to the Larger Vision

The organizational change that transpired in the Methodist Church to eliminate the Central Jurisdiction teaches us *change involves connecting the transition to the broader vision, the ultimate goal.* Organizational change is challenging, particularly when you are trying to change attitudes and behaviors. Some people think nothing new is needed (Qian, 2007). Some people do not want to learn anything new.

Others are institutionalized, which Agocs (1997) called institutionalized resistance. This type of resistance means the methods leaders will use "to actively deny, reject, refuse to implement, repress, or even dismantle change proposals and initiatives" (p. 918). Agocs argued that there are four forms of resistance: "denial of the need for change, refusal to accept responsibility for dealing with the change issue, refusal to implement change that has been agreed to, and action to dismantle change that has been initiated" (p. 920). With the difficulty of organizational change, change agents can get discouraged and lose sight of the silver lining (Qian, 2007). Thus, your leadership must connect the changes to the broader vision. How is this accomplished?

First, your leaders need to make sure stakeholders understand there are high dividends to the organizational changes. They must realize that change will benefit the heart of your business: your image and purpose. **Second,** the message for change needs to be about your organization's outcomes. Focusing on the results will help your organization consistently measure your business's progress. It will also keep your team from becoming distracted. It will help your organization be accountable for every decision and course of action taken. **Third,** connect the changes to the larger vision by aligning your organizational strategy, values, and priorities. There needs to be a cohesive, aligned message that empowers your leaders and followers to understand how changing will enhance the organization (Qian, 2007). Without these corresponding messages, your team will be reluctant to take the steps forward so that they can grow.

Paul implemented similar steps in the Galatian church. He knew the people were concerned about being the church that God had called them to be. He told them they could not be that church without including everyone, understanding that everyone was necessary, and understanding that no part of the Body of Christ was more important than the others.

In the Methodist Church, those who sought to bring about an age of enlightenment by dismantling the Central Jurisdiction understood that many in the Methodist denomination wanted to be the Church God had called the followers of Jesus to be. Therefore, it appears that those who desired to change the organizational structure sought to connect the message of change to the broader vision: being the true Body of Christ. They built their herculean effort and inexorable march for equity around this theme.

We see this cleverly demonstrated in Dr. Matthew Simpson Davage's presentation to the 1939 Uniting Conference (Thomas, 1992). Even though most of the African Americans intended to vote against the Plan of Union, which excluded them, Dr. Davage thought it was best to move forward with the Methodist Church's proposal; vote on it, and pass it, looking to a brighter day. That day, when Dr. Davage, with his keen insight, made his speech, he cleverly connected the proposal to the Church's broader vision. This vision that the people were concerned about was being the true church of Jesus Christ. "There is no longer Jew or Greek, there is no longer slave or free, there is no longer male or female; for all of you are one in Christ Jesus" (Gal. 3:28, English Standard Version). Dr. Davage said,

> I am for it. The proposed Plan of Unification . . . is not a perfect instrument—and . . . it does not wholly satisfy the desires of any single group. In making our decisions this day we are not called upon to agree that the thing proposed is perfect, but to decide whether or not this endeavor to bridge the gap between this ultimate ideal and the immediately possible reality is a step in the direction of one-fold and one Shepherd. ("Methodist Episcopal Church," 1936, p. 88)

Dr. Davage did not make his speech about a present change but instead about the outcome (Thomas, 1992). He made it about one step, or two, in the right direction of becoming one flock with one Shepherd, Jesus Christ. It was almost as if he were saying, "This is a part of the process of becoming that one true church. Change is coming, and this Central Jurisdictional structure, which many of us are adamantly against, is a part of getting us to our ultimate destiny."

The larger vision, as seen by the Central Jurisdiction, not only had to do with becoming one flock with one Shepherd but also becoming God's Methodist children in one Church. We can see the goal of being one flock and God's Methodist children with one shepherd in this question that people inside and outside the Church asked so many times: why did so many stay in the Methodist Church? For the African Americans who stayed, this represented their way of connecting to the broader vision. Bishop Thomas (1992) said, "Why not give racial inclusion relations a chance to prove itself to be workable in the church?" (p. 52).

Bishop Willis J. King also helps us see the larger vision. He elucidated that what was ultimately crucial to African Americans, more than rights and privileges, was that the Methodist Church showed from its inception that the fellowship embodied a relationship that was earnestly striving for unity among all people (Thomas, 1992). He further said that African Americans believed their presence in such a church would help God accomplish that ultimate goal of having his Methodist children in one Church.

William McClain (1984) concluded that a considerable measure of why African Americans remained in the Church was because of hope. Their persistent faith propelled them. Their anticipation of what the Church would be was not rooted in the soil of what they were presently seeing. Instead, their drive was rooted in pride, hope, and faith that God would make a way somehow; that people would not see their presence as a glitch in the system but as God's providence. Although staying in the Methodist Church was an emotional seesaw, Blacks would not allow the Church to drain them of their hope or pride.

We learn the following from connecting the change to the broader vision: **One**, connecting your business's growth to your organization's more overall vision is vitally important for the transition to be successful. **Two,** it will help you overcome obstacles and help you persevere when times get challenging. **Three**, regardless of the struggles and the adversities, connecting the change to your company's broader vision will allow you always to keep before you what you are asking and why you are laboring for growth. **Last,** linking your company's transformation to the larger purpose will keep your team focused and inspired.

REVIEW QUESTIONS

1. What does Paul's travels to Galatia and Corinth teach us about change?
2. What are the two kinds of changes highlighted by Mennella and Strayer?
3. List and explain the five models of change that organizations can use to transform organizational culture.
4. What change model was used to abolish the Central Jurisdiction?

5. In the stages of the Lewin model of change as it relates to the Central Jurisdiction, what do you learn about organizational evolution?
6. Who were considered change agents during the Methodist Reformation?
7. What three organizational change lessons did you learn?

Chapter 5
CONCLUSION: WHERE DO YOU START?

LEARNING OBJECTIVES

- Explain why organizational change is necessary.
- Explain why people fear change.
- Define Wiener's definition of organizational readiness.
- Explain the role an organization's DNA plays in keeping an organization from changing.
- Explain what an organization needs to do to be a successful organization.
- Discuss the nine keys to organizational change.
- Discuss why words need to match actions.

ORGANIZATIONAL CHANGE FOR ANY BUSINESS IS ESSENTIAL IF it expects to thrive and be relevant in the future. Change is a continual process for any organization that hopes to survive. Many organizations, such as Blockbuster, Sears, and Pan American World Airways, were the leading organizations of their time but do not exist today because they did not embrace changes in the environment. Change is everlasting, and those organizations that do not get a hold of this concept will not experience innovative success but will perpetually fail and eventually face extinction. This chapter highlights where your organization needs to start to implement change. It emphasizes the necessary steps for accomplishing positive, productive, and progressive structural and cultural transformation.

LEARN REASONS FOR CHANGE

Your leaders need to understand that there is no solid reason that your institution may need to make changes. Your organization may need to change for various reasons: technological evolution, revenue growth, crisis, improved customer satisfaction, customers' change of habits, environmental changes, enhanced quality of life, business process, and so on (Kotter, 1996). It may be necessary for your organization to make changes because your leadership team may need to redirect resources.

Looking at your organization's current practice, your organization's philosophy and values may require changes, and you may need to adjust your plans. Your business may need new ideas because your establishment location could be experiencing racial and ethnic transitioning. Environments are dynamic, which means your organization must be responsive to these environments if you expect to survive.

It may be that your organization must change because there is a gap between what your institution expects and what your leaders are accomplishing. Times will arise when entrepreneurs introduce new technologies into society. For your organization to be competitive, your business will have to adapt, or thriving companies will force your establishment out of business. Your team might need to evolve because of internal and external pressures, as we saw with the Methodist organization. Whatever the reason, one of your paramount goals will be to understand what is driving the need for change in your establishment.

LEARN REASONS PEOPLE FEAR CHANGE

You will discover, if you have not already, that changing organizational culture is backbreaking. Some of your corporate leaders and members will not accept change easily or readily. It is not that they are merely trying to be cantankerous, but they may resist change because they fear losing things they value, such as influence, power, and values.

Sometimes, some people might fear what they have to lose instead of what they have to gain in the change process. They might fear losing control over their affairs, authority, and knowledge. Sweeney and McFarlin (2002) noted that knowledge is power, and change can overturn that knowledge, then take power away. Therefore, some people may feel that evolving deprives them of knowing and controlling their future.

Not only may there be a fear of change that keeps your establishment from moving to a new day, but also your institution's organizational readiness levels may be low. Wiener (2009) defined organizational readiness for change as "organizational members' shared resolve to implement a change (change commitment) and shared belief in their collective capability to do so (change efficacy)" (para. 2). When your business's shared resolve for change and the shared belief that change is possible are low, the change will be difficult, if not impossible.

Moreover, your organizational change might be difficult because your corporate members may be unable to see better ways to face the future. They would rather stay as they are. They would rather have members conform than create (McClain, 1984).

Whether it is a local church, a denomination, a school, or a business, organizational culture has an embedded array of aspirations, functions, networks, policies, morals, attitudes, traditions, and notions. These systems are the corporate culture's personality or DNA. As Peter F. Drucker (1959) said, "culture eats strategy for breakfast" (p. 28). These systems are interlocked to protect and defend your organization's present system. Still, if you apply the principles offered in this book, you will be able to confront the interlocks successfully.

LEARN ORGANIZATIONAL LESSONS FOR SUCCESSFUL ORGANIZATIONAL CHANGE

Your organization can change for the better if you learn and apply the nine keys discussed in this book: (a) establish a transformational team; (b) study how plans develop; (c) learn and choose

Conclusion: Where Do You Start?

a model of change; (d) select change agents with courage; (e) set goals and priorities for the change team; (f) challenge the organizational ethos, direction, and ambitions; (g) choose innovative leadership to put into words the vision; (h) overcome opposition to change; and (i) connect the transformation to the larger idea. The process of the Central Jurisdiction's abolishment clarifies that leaders of change must help all involved see a vision that will make them and the organization more productive. The leaders must also assist the organization in producing better people and thereby a better world. Helping others to connect to the vision that an organizational overhaul is needed is the trigger to change.

These nine steps will improve your business's ability to compete, succeed, and perform more effectively. As your organization develops as you study the concepts in this book—knowing when, how, and why to implement change—you will take on your new opportunity for growth with excitement. Your leaders will be able to create an environment for change. They will undoubtedly be able to discuss with others who are a part of your organization why your business needs to change.

These nine steps will help your organization successfully deal with the fears and resistance of change. Learning these steps will aid you in reducing organizational disruptions. It will also help you minimize confusion and uncertainty for people as your organization journeys toward your promised land of milk and honey: fertility, delight, and abundance.

SHARE THE IMPACT OF ORGANIZATIONAL CHANGE

As you seek to change your organization for the better, you must answer these questions and share the answers with others as often as you can:

- How are the changes that are put in place today going to help achieve your organizational vision for tomorrow?
- What will the impact of the organizational change be on the organization's future?

As I have tried to restate through this book repeatedly, the change process is no easy feat; it is uncertain at times, stressful, and risky. But frequently as possible, articulating the positive impact of the changes will strengthen your case for change. The Methodist Church transformation process to remove the Central Jurisdiction demonstrates that an exact meaning or purpose behind the change will help build a better understanding of the change strategy. It will also make reasons for the change more compelling.

For your followers or employees or stockholders to understand what is in the transition for them, how the change will positively impact their lives and communities will strengthen your case for change and get more buy-in from those whom the change will affect. According to the *Merriam-Webster Dictionary*, buy-in means to accept and be willing to actively support and play a part in something, such as a project, mission, or plan. Regardless of who leads or what the vision is, it takes procuring support at all organizational levels. To gain that canvass of support, convey to your organizational members what things will look like when the governing body has executed the change.

MATCH YOUR WORDS WITH YOUR ACTIONS

With the Vietnam War, the assassination of John F. Kennedy on November 22, 1963, the assassination of Malcolm X on February 21, 1965, and the assassination of Dr. Martin Luther King, Jr, in April 1968, the world seemed to be crumbling. However, there was a glimmer of hope. After forces of change, many years of protest, blood, sweat, and tears, they finally dealt a fatal blow to the body of the racially structured paradigm. The Methodist organization finally passed a constitutional amendment declaring that by 1972 all UMC racial structures would be eliminated.

The MEC that Methodist people organized under Thomas Coke's and Francis Asbury's leadership in 1784 in Baltimore, Maryland, that divided over slavery in 1844, and that reunited in 1939 was about to grab hands as a unified church. After almost 30 years, after the MEC agreed that the 1939 reunion could take place with the stipulation that the Church had to place African Americans in a separate racially structured jurisdiction, the Methodist Church, amid the howling chaos of the 1960s, was finally exiting from the jungles of segregation. It was a protracted taxing battle, but the Methodist members who supported an integrated church did not let the fight dim their star. With their resourcefulness and gutsy determination, they marched onward to Zion—at least the Zion they felt existed on this earth. A satisfying soul event was about to take place. A new day was about to make its first appearance from behind the curtains.

During the ambience of festivity and high voltage gathering of the 1968 General Conference, the Methodist organization, with its 10.3 million members, and the EUB with its 750,000 members signed, sealed, and delivered the merger (The People of the United Methodist Church, 2018). Following various, long and crowded meetings and crushing disappointments, the transformational leaders and change agents had finally reached the hearts and awakened the souls of the resisters to change. After the daunting and lingering challenges and deep dark wells of sorrow, the Central Jurisdiction was finally fading away like a cloud on the horizon. Nearer than ever before was the end. It was like listening to a pleasant tune.

With all of its gifted intelligence, gushing enthusiasm, and glowing anticipation, the all-African American jurisdiction's plans for a more just future was about to bear fruit. The Methodist Church was on the verge of putting into practice what Abraham Lincoln sought to do for Black people in secular society when he signed the *Emancipation Proclamation*: to provide all of its members with an "open field and fair chance to use their industry, enterprise, and intelligence; that you may all have equal privileges in the race of life, with all its desirable human aspirations" (A. Lincoln, 2018, para. 3).

All that had predated April 23, 1968, was, in the beginning, a means to an end. That end was the recreation of the Methodist Church itself. A welcome sign was raised and flown in every Black Methodist's heart for the end of a system meant to degrade African Americans and chord them off from Caucasians as if Blacks were animals to be caged, fed, and trained. Once again, God breathed across the abyss and set the captives free:

Conclusion: Where Do You Start?

On April 23, 1968, two bishops followed by two children, two youths, two adults, six ordained ministers, two church officers and finally all 10,000 people present joined hands and repeated in unison:

"Lord of the church, we are united in thee, in thy church, and now in The United Methodist Church. Amen." (Hahn, 2018)

This merger terminated the existence of the Central Jurisdiction. Until it was cremated and poured into the urns of history, the racially structured jurisdiction had life for almost 30 years. Both denominations—The Methodist Church and the Evangelical United Brethren Church—adopted a constitutional paragraph requiring that "no conference or other organizational unit of the church shall be structured so as to exclude any member or any constituent body of the church because of race" ("The Judicial Council Re-affirms," 1966, 852).

According to McEllhenney et al. (1992), the strategy that established the United Methodist Church in 1968 deleted the Central Jurisdiction and dodged the fact that Methodism had a jurisdiction based on race. Although the Church steered clear of mentioning the racial jurisdiction, "separate African American annual conferences continued on into the early 1970s" (McEllhenney et al., 1992, p. 121).

Although both denominations adopted a policy that stated that no structure would have life in the Methodist Church that would shut out members based on race, this change of direction took some time to implement. Also, to make sure that the change did not unravel and continue to move forward, the church established the

Lessons from the Methodist Reformation that Will Transform Any Organization

Commission on Religion and Race. This commission exists to this day to advocate for inclusion in every area of the church.

As you move toward your brighter days, remember growth will not happen overnight. Change is a process, not an event. It will happen step by step, as your organization changes its heart, changes its mind, and executes the action the organizational process underscores in this book.

The Central Jurisdiction's leaders and others who wanted a change in the Methodist organization made it loud and clear what needed to be changed. The Central Jurisdiction based their assessment on the kind of institution the Methodist organization said it was and how it was portraying itself. The organization was saying one thing and doing another. Therefore, they had to align their actions with their words.

The result was not a church with no frivolous and fussy interiors. No institution is without some drama. The outcome was not an institution without a scratch (because no institution or person is perfect). Instead, the result was a better performing institution with blazing global power, astonishing dimensions, and divine instinct uplifting souls as on dovelike wings.

The United Methodist organization is now a global connectional church. It is an organization filled with people of various races, colors, and genders from 60 countries working as a team feeding the hungry, clothing the naked, and being eyes to the blind.

One of the things that successful organizations do is decorate their business with furniture that reflects their personality. Your organization will have to do the same. In other words, your organization will need to look at who you presently are and what you want to be and then move into position and place your organization's behaviors parallel with their expressions.

Your leaders will have to take a critical look at the kind of institution you are now and how you show and tell that image. Your business will also need to look at its written vision statement and answer these five questions:

- Is this who we are?
- If this is not who we are, how do we become the organization we claim to be?
- What do we need to keep?
- What do we need to remove?
- What do we need to strengthen or improve?

Taking a critical review of who you presently are and what you want to be using the five questions above will help ignite the change you want to achieve. Your words communicate how you want people to see your organization. Your actions prove who you are. Institutions, businesses, and companies whose values do not match their actions are unhealthy and not as productive as possible.

If your organization is saying one thing and doing another, your organization is in critical condition and on life support. It is not performing at its peak. You can change this by gathering your present leaders and some of your customers and discussing the five questions above. Then your organization will need to put into action the lessons that you learned from the Reformation that changed the Methodist organization. As you implement what you have learned in this book, your organization will begin to boom. This book will teach you that your business or group or team will have to throw

Lessons from the Methodist Reformation that Will Transform Any Organization

out some of your old ways to earn the best days of your organization's life. However, every challenge, every loss, every cascading tear, every bit of the uphill struggle will be worth it in the end.

REVIEW QUESTIONS

1. Why do organizations have to change?
2. Why do people dread change?
3. What is Wiener's definition of organizational readiness?
4. What is the meaning of corporate DNA?
5. What drives organizational success?
6. What are the nine steps to organizational change?

ACKNOWLEDGMENTS

FOR THE INVALUABLE INSIGHTS, ENCOURAGEMENT, CONVERSAtion, criticism, and other assistance, I am grateful for my wife, Dr. Zina Rhodes, and my son Steven Rhodes. I am grateful for the invaluable feedback from Bishop Alfred Norris, a retired Bishop in the United Methodist Church.

I want to thank Dr. Mary Jo Burchard, for encouraging me during my Ph.D. dissertation process to write this book.

I am thankful for the Methodist Reformation that unstitched the Central Jurisdiction from the fabric of its cloth. I am grateful for that dazzling display of combustible energy expended by Methodism's forefathers and mothers to make the Church a better organization.

Grateful am I to those who looked into the faces of an array of antagonists and did not throw in the towel. The metamorphosis through which Methodism has gone is a success story to be praised. Because of the faith of unseen things and the will of the Central Jurisdiction, and others, the Methodist Church seeks to craft a future based on equality and justice. Although the battle still rages on for fairness, I represent the end goal of those who fought injustice, separation, and the Church's racial dilemma. I am the fruit of their labor.

I am thankful that God spoke to the Methodist organization and the Central Jurisdiction, conveying that people are different. Nevertheless, different traditions, cultures, languages, foods, and behaviors do not mean we cannot work together to make the world a healthier, more peaceful, and caring place. Our differences are strengths, not weaknesses. They are our beauty.

I am also thankful to the leadership in the Central Jurisdiction for agitating for change. Like others, they could have resigned from the Methodist organization. But instead, they chose to stay. And I am eternally grateful because if they had decided to leave, perhaps they would not have produced this leader.

My sincerest thanks to the Central Jurisdiction and others who were internal and external agents of change. I realize that my horizons of opportunities and possibilities in the United Methodist Organization did not roll in on tender and docile waves. I am the product of many selfless sacrifices of those who did not opt to be marginalized beggars but fought for full participation for African Americans in the Methodist Church. I am the product of the ultimate goal of those who wear their wounds like stars. I am a product (and there are many others) of those who agitate and advocate for the organization's broader vision, now called the United Methodist Church.

Thank God for the Methodist Church's change agents' heroic fortitude for not settling for the dimmest and quietest token gestures of inclusion. We are now, both Black people and White, together in the same Church. We are not perfect. However, we changed for the better, and we are a long way from what we were in 1939. The process of organizational change experienced in the Methodist Church to rid itself of the Central Jurisdiction has much to offer other organizations.

If any organization takes those differences, agitates, and advocates for constructive change when the organization's ambitions and procedures do not portray who the organization is; excavates the best-shared ideas; and implements and builds upon them, the organization can be successful. The Methodist Reformation that transformed the Methodist Church into the United Methodist Church demonstrates that earthshaking change can sprout in any institution. Any organization that marshals the most substantial reasons for change, unifies, creates a vision, and works together toward the idea that institution will not die; it will become a powerful, productive, and dynamic organization because teamwork makes the dream work.

REFERENCES

Adams, J. S. (1963). Toward an understanding of inequity. *Journal of Abnormal Social Psychology, 67*(5), 422-436. Retrieved from https://doi.org/ 10.1037/ h0040968

Adams, J. S. (1965). Inequity in social exchange. In L. Berkowitz (Ed.), *Advances in experimental social psychology* (Vol. 2, pp. 267-299). New York, NY: Academic.

Agocs, C. (1997). *Institutionalized resistance to organizational change: Denial, inaction, and repression. Journal of Business Ethics, 16, 917-931.*

Allen, J. L. (1963). The Methodist Union in the United States. In N. Ehrenstrom & W. G. Muelder. *Institutionalism and church unity* (p. 284). New York, NY: Association Press.

Amos, B., & Kilmoski, R. (2014). Courage: Making teamwork work well. *Group & Organization Management, 39*(1), 110-128, Retrieved from https://doi.org/10.1177/1059601113520407

Armenakis, A. A., Harris, S. G., & Feild, H. S. (1999). Making change permanent: A model for institutionalizing change. In W. Pasmore & R. Woodman (Eds.), *Research in organization change and development* (Vol. 12, pp. 97-128). Greenwich, CT: JAI Press.

Backer, T. E. (1995). Assessing and enhancing readiness for change: Implications for technology transfer. In T. E. Backer, S. L. David, & G. Saucy (Eds.), *Reviewing the Behavioral Science Knowledge Base on Technology Transfer* (Monograph No. 155; pp. 21-40). Retrieved from https://archives.drugabuse.gov/sites/ default/files/monograph155.pdf

Bandura, A. (1977). Self-efficacy: Toward a unifying theory of behavioral change. *Psychological Review, 84*(2), 191-215.

Bandura, A. (1986). *Social foundations of thought and action: A social cognitive theory*. Englewood Cliffs, NJ: Prentice-Hall.

Bandura, A. (Ed.) (1995). *Self-efficacy in changing societies*. Cambridge, United Kingdom: Cambridge University Press.

Bandura, A. (1997). *Self-efficacy: The exercise of control*. New York, NY: W. H. Freeman.

Banford, D., & Daniel, S. (2005). A case study of change management effectiveness within the NHS. *Journal of Change Management, 5*(4), 391-406. Retrieved from https://doi.org/10.1080/14697010500287360

Barnett, W. P., & Carroll, G. R. (1995). Modeling internal organizational change. *Annual Review of Sociology, 21*, 217-236. Retrieved from https://doi.org/10.1146/annurev.so.21.080195.001245

Barrett, F. J., Thomas, G. F., & Hocevar, S. (1995). The central role of discourse in largescale change: A social construction perspective. *The Journal of Applied Behavioral Science, 31*(3), 352-372. Retrieved from https://doi.org/10.1177/0021886395313007

Bass, B. M., & Bass, R. (2008). *The Bass handbook of leadership: Theory, research, and managerial applications*. New York, NY: Free Press.

Bass, B. M., & Riggio, R. E. (2006). *Transformational leadership* (2nd ed.). New York, NY: Psychology Press.

Beckhard, R. (1969). *Agent of change, my life, my practice*. Los Angeles, CA: Jossey-Bass.

Bederman, G. (1995). *Manliness and civilization: A cultural history of gender and race in the United States, 1880-1917*. Chicago, IL: University of Chicago.

References

Beer, M., & Walton, A. E. (1987). Organization change and development. *Annual Review of Psychology, 38*(1), 339-367.

Bennett, J. B. (2005). *Religion and the rise of Jim Crow in New Orleans.* Princeton, NJ: Princeton University.

Bennis, W. On becoming a leader (4th ed.). New York, Basic Books.

Bernerth, J. (2004). Expanding our understanding of the change message. *Human Resource Development Review, 3*(1), 36-52.

Bertalanffy, L. V. (1968). *General systems theory: Foundations, development, applications.* New York, NY: Braziller.

Best, P. W. (1994). *Locus of control, personal commitment and commitment to the organisation* (Unpublished thesis). University of South Africa, Pretoria.

Bouckenooghe, D., Schwarz, G., M., & Minbashian, A. (2015). *Herscovitch and Meyer's three-component model of commitment to change: Meta-analytic findings. European Journal of Work and Organizational Psychology, 24(4), 578-595.* doi:10.1080/1359432X.2014.963059

Brawley, J. P. (1967, October 15). Methodist Church from 1939. *Central Christian Advocate*, p. 3.

Buffett, W. (n.d.). *Warren Buffett quotes.* Retrieved from https://www.brainyquote.com/quotes/warren_buffett_409214

Burke, W. W., & Litwin, G. H. (1992). A causal model of organizational performance and change. *Journal of Management, 18*(3), 523-545. Retrieved from https://doi.org/10.1177/ 014920639201800306

Burnes, B., & By, R. T. (2012). Leadership and change: The case for greater ethical clarity. *Journal of Business Ethics, 10*(8), 239-252. doi:10.1007/s10551-011-1088-2

Burns, J. M. (1978). *Leadership.* New York, NY: Harper & Row.

Caldwell, G. (2012, August 17). *Church history requires we discuss racism*. Retrieved from https://www.umnews.org/en/news/church- history-requires-we-discuss-racism

Cameron, E., & Green, M. (2008). *Making sense of leadership: Exploring the five key roles used by effective leaders*. London, United Kingdom: Kogan Page.

Carney, M. P. (1999). *The human side of organizational change: Evolution, adaption, and emotional intelligence, a formula for success* (Unpublished doctoral dissertation). Widener University, Chester, PA.

Cawsey, T., Deszca, G., & Ingols, C. (2012). *Organizational change: An action-oriented toolkit* (2nd ed.). Thousand Oaks, CA: SAGE.

Church segregation denounced by bishops. (1964, January 1). *Central Christian Advocate, 139*(1), 3.

Cochran, J. K., Bromley, M. L., & Swando, M. J. (2002). Sheriff's deputies' receptivity to organizational change. *Policing: An International Journal, 25*(3), 507-530. Retrieved from https://doi.org/10.1108/13639510210437014

Coeling, H. V., & Simms, L. M. (1993). Facilitating innovation at the nursing unit level through cultural assessment, Part 1: How to keep management ideas from falling on deaf ears. *Journal of Nursing Administration, 23*(4), 46-53. doi:10.1097/00005110-199304000-00013

Cohen, S., & Bailey, D. E. (1997). What makes teams work: Group effectiveness research from the shop floor to the executive suite. *Journal of Management, 23*(3), 239-290. Retrieved from https://doi.org/10.1016/S0149-2063(97)90034-9

Collins, J. (2001). *Good to great*. New York, NY: HarperCollins.

Cranston, E. (2011). *Breaking down the walls: A contribution to Methodist unification*. Charleston, SC: Nabu Press.

Cummings, T., & Worley, C. (2008). *Organizational development and change* (9th ed.). Mason, OH: South-Western Cengage Learning.

Cunningham, C. E., Woodward, C. A., Shannon, H. S., MacIntosh, J., Lendrum, B., Rosenbloom, D., & Brown, J. (2002). Readiness for organizational change: A longitudinal study of workplace, psychological and behavioural correlates. *Journal of Occupational & Organizational Psychology, 75*(4), 377-392.

Darling, P. (1993). Getting results: The trainer's skills. *Management Development Review, 6*(5), 25-29. Retrieved from https://doi.org/10.1108/EUM0000000000757

Davis, M. L. (2008). *The Methodist unification: Christianity and the politics of race in the Jim Crow era.* New York: New York University Press.

Desplaces, D. (2005). A multilevel approach to individual readiness to change. *Journal of Behavioral and Applied Management, 7*(1), 25-39. doi:10.21818/001c.14568

Dickson, M. W., Aditya, R. N., & Chhokar, J. S. (2000). Definition and interpretation in cross-cultural organizational culture research. In N. M. Ashkanasy, C. P. Wilderom, & M. F. Peterson (Eds.), *Handbook of organizational culture and climate* (pp. 447-464). Thousand Oaks, CA: SAGE.

Disney, R. E. (n.d.). *Roy E. Disney quotes.* Retrieved from https://www.brainyquote.com/quotes/roy_e_disney_170949

Display advertisement #105. (1963, October 7). *New York Times*, p. 26.

Dolan, V. (2011). The isolation of online adjunct faculty and its impact on their performance. *The International Review of Research in Open and Distance Learning, 12*(2), 1-9. Retrieved from https://doi.org/10.19173/irrodl.v12i2.793

Drucker, P. (1954). *The practice of management.* New York, NY: Harper and Row.

Drucker, P. F. (*1959*). Work and tools. *Technology and Culture, 1*(1), 28-37. doi:10.2307/3100785

Dunmore, D. (2013). *Has technology become a need? A qualitative study exploring three generational cohorts' perception of technology in regards to Maslow's hierarchy of needs* (Doctoral dissertation). Available from ProQuest Dissertations and Theses database. (UMI No. 3607006)

Episcopal Address. (April 27, 1964). *Daily Christian Advocate*, p. *15.*

Evans, R. (1982). *Resistance to innovations in information technology in higher education: A social psychological perspective.* In B. Sheehan (Ed.), *Information technology: Innovations and applications* (pp. 89-103). San Francisco, CA: Jossey-Bass.

Falconer, J. (2001). Business patterns as knowledge augmentation metaphor: The research frame of organizational change. In N. Bontis & C. Bart (Eds.), *Proceedings of the 4th World Congress on Management of Intellectual Capital.* Hamilton, Ontario: McMaster University.

Flamholtz, E., & Randle, Y. (2008). *Leading strategic change: Bridging theory and practice.* Cambridge, United Kingdom: Cambridge University Press.

Frank, T. (2006) *Polity, practice, and the mission of the United Methodist Church* (2nd ed.). Nashville, TN: Abingdon.

Frankenberg, R. (1993). *White women, race matters.* Minneapolis: University of Minnesota.

Frazier, N. (2017). Harambee City: The congress of racial equality in Cleveland and the rise of Black power populism. Fayetteville: University of Arkansas Press.

Gandhi, M. (n.d.). *Mahatma Gandhi quotes.* Retrieved from http://www.notable-quotes.com/g/gandhi_mahatma.html

Gardner, J. W. (1995). Self-renewal: The individual and the innovative society. New York, NY: Norton.

References

Gardner, P. J. (2009). Organizational change: All we want is better projects—Why so difficult? *AACE International Transactions*, 1-25. Retrieved from https://changemanagementguide.files. wordpress.com/2010/10/48225949.pdf

General Conference of 1952. (1952, April 24). *Daily Christian Advocate, 64*, 64.

General Conference of 1956. (April 26, 1956). *Daily Christian Advocate, p. 85.*

Gist, M. E., & Mitchell, T. R. (1992). Self-efficacy: A theoretical analysis of its determinants and malleability. *Academy of Management Review, 17*(2), 183-211.

Glaude, E. S., Jr. (2016). *Democracy in Black: How race still enslaves the American soul*. New York, NY. Broadway Books.Goldstone, L. (2011). *Inherently unequal: The betrayal of equal rights by the Supreme Court, 1865-1903*. London, United Kingdom: Walker Books.

Goodwin, D. K. (2018). *Leadership in turbulent times*. New York, NY: Simon & Schuster.

Griffith, T. L. (2002). Why change management fails. *Journal of Management, 2*(4), 297-305. Retrieved from https://doi.org/ 10.1080/714042516

Hahn, H. (2018). *Amid tumult of 1968, a church came together*. Retrieved from https://www.umnews.org/en/news/amid-tumult-of-1968-a-church-came-together

Hammer, M., & Champy. J. (2006). Reengineering the corporation: A Manifesto for business revolution (Collins Business Essentials). New York: HarperCollins.

Hargis, M. B., Wyatt, J. D., & Piotrowski, C. (2001). Developing leaders: Examining the role of transactional and transformational leadership across contexts. *Business Organization Development Journal, 29*(3), 51-66.

Harvey, T. R., & Broyles, E. A. (2010). *Resistance to change: A guide to harnessing its positive power*. Lanham, MD: Rowman & Littlefield Education.

Haskins, J. (1999). *Rosa Parks: My story*. London, United Kingdom: Puffin Books.

Heifetz, R. A., & Linsky, M. (2004). When leadership spells danger. *Educational Leadership, 61*(7), 33-37. Retrieved from http://www.faithformation-learningexchange.net/uploads/5/2/4/6/5246709/_ronald_a._heifetz_and_marty_linsky.pdf

Hiatt, J. M. (2006). *ADKAR: A model for change in business, government and our community*. Loveland, CO: Prosci.

Hiatt, J. M., & Creasey, T. J. (2012). *Change management: The people side of change*. Loveland, CO: Prosci.

Higgs, M., & Rowland, D. (2005). All changes great and small: Exploring approaches to change and its leadership. *Journal of Change Management, 5*(2), 121-151. Retrieved from https://doi.org/10.1080/14697010500082902

Houck, D., & Dixon, D. E. (2009). *Women and the civil rights movement, 1954-1965*. Jackson: University Press of Mississippi.

Hsiang, C. (2002). *Relationships of teamwork skills with performance appraisals and salary information in a Taiwanese high-performance work organization* (Doctoral dissertation). Available from ProQuest Dissertations and Theses database. (UMI No. 3094314)

Huff, A. V., Jr. (2016). *Southern Methodist Church*. Retrieved from http://www.scencyclopedia.org/sce/entries/southern-methodist-church/

Irvin, D. L. (1992). *Unsung heart of Black America: A middle-class church at Midcentury*. Columbia: University of Missouri Press.

Jerome, N. (2013). Application of the Maslow's hierarchy of need theory; impacts and implications on organizational culture, human resource and employee's performance. *International Journal of Business and Management Invention, 1*(3), 39-35. Retrieved from https://pdfs.semanticscholar.org/b0bc/c8ca-45193eaf700350a8ac2ddfc09a093be8.pdf

Jick, T. D., & Peiperl, M. A. (1998). *Managing change: Cases and concepts* (2nd ed.). Boston, MD: McGraw-Hill Education.

Jones, R. A., Jimmieson, N. L., & Griffiths, A. (2005). The impact of organizational culture and reshaping capabilities on change implementation success: The mediating role of readiness for change. *Journal of Management Studies, 42*(2), 361-386.

Journal of the Sixth Session of the Central Jurisdiction of the Methodist Church. (1960). p. 138.

The Judicial Council re-affirms no deadline decision. (1966). Judicial Council Decision, 852.

Jung, D. D., & Sosik, J. J. (2002). Transformational leadership in work groups: The role of empowerment, cohesiveness, and collective-efficacy on perceived group performance. *Small Group Research, 33*, 313-336.

Keller, H. (n.d.). *25 inspirational Helen Keller quotes on happiness, vision and purpose.* Retrieved from https://www.goalcast.com/2019/01/31/helen-keller-quotes/

Keller, R. S., Ruether, R. R., & Cantlon, M. (2006). *Encyclopedia of women and religion in North America.* Bloomington: Indiana University.

Kerber, K. W. & Buono, A. F. (Ed.). (2010). Intervention and organizational change: Building organizational change capacity. In A. F. Buono (Ed.) *An evolving paradigm: Integrative perspectives on organizational development, change, strategic management, and ethics* (pp. 181-212). Charlotte, NC: Information Age.

Kets de Vries, M. F. R. (Ed.). (1991). *Organizations on the couch.* San Francisco, CA: Jossey-Bass.

Kets de Vries. (2006). *Leader on the couch: A clinical approach to changing people and organizations.* West Sussex, England: John Wiley & Sons.

King, M. L., Jr. (1986). I have a dream. In J. M. Washington (Ed.), *The essential writings and speeches of Martin Luther King, Jr.* (pp. 217-220). San Francisco, CA: HarperCollins.

Kirk, A. W. (2005). *Desegregation of the Methodist Church polity: Reform movements that ended racial segregation*. Pittsburgh, PA: RoseDog.

Klein, A. (2011). Thin coffers, ambitious education agendas put newly elected leaders on spot. *Education Week, 30*(16), 37-38. Retrieved from https://www.edweek.org/ew/articles/2011/ 01/13/16politics.h30.html

Kotter, J. P. (1990). *A force for change: How leadership differs from management*. New York, NY: Free Press.

Kotter, J. P. (1996). *Leading change*. Cambridge, MA: Harvard Business School Press.

Kotter, J. P., & Heskett, J. L. (1992). *Corporate culture and performance*. New York, NY: Free Press.

Kotter, J. P., & Schlesinger, L. A. (2008). Choosing strategies for change. *Harvard Business Review, 86* (7-8), 451-459. Retrieved from https://projects.iq.harvard.edu/files/sdpfellowship/files/ day3_2_choosing_strategies_for_change.pdf

Kübler-Ross, E., & Kessler, D. (2014). *On grief & grieving: Finding the meaning of grief through the five stages of loss*. New York, NY: Scribner.

Lawler, E. E., III. (1986). *High involvement management. Participative strategies for improving organizational performance*. San Francisco, CA: Jossey-Bass.

Lee, R., & Miller, T. (2001). Evaluating the performance of the Lee-Carter approach to modeling and forecasting mortality. *Demography, 38*(4), 537-549.

Leslie, L., Park, T., & Mehng, S. (2012). Flexible work practice: A source of career premiums or penalty. *Academy of Management Journal, 55*(6), 1407-1428. https://dx.doi.org/10.5465/amj. 2010.0651

Lewin, K. (1951). Problems of research in social psychology. In D. Cartwright. (Eds), *Field theory in social science* (p. 346). New York, NY: Harper & Row.

References

Lewis, L. K., Laster, N., & Kulkarni, V. (2013). Telling 'em how it will be: Previewing pain risky change in initial announcements. *International Journal of Business Communication*, *50*(3), 278-308. https://doi.org/10.1177/0021943613487072

Lincoln, A. (2018). *Abraham Lincoln's speeches to Ohio regiments*. Retrieved from http://www.abrahamlincolnonline.org/lincoln/ speeches/ohio.htm

Lincoln, C. E. (1967). *The Negro pilgrimages in America*. New York, NY: Bantam Books.

Lowe, G. (2012). *Creating healthy organizations: How vibrant workplaces inspire employees to achieve sustainable success*. Toronto, Ontario: Rotman-UTP.

Lowery, J. (1966). *Remarks by Dr. Lowery. The Daily Advocate*, 851.

Lunenburg, F. C. (2011). Expectancy theory of motivation: Motivating by altering expectations. *International Journal of Management, Business, and Administration*, *15*(1), 1-6. Retrieved from http://www.nationalforum.com/Electronic% 20Journal%20Volumes/Luneneburg,%20Fred%20 C%20Expectancy%20Theory%20%20Altering%20Expectations%20 IJMBA%20V 15%20N1%202011.pdf

Mandela, N. (n.d.). *Nelson Mandela quotes*. Retrieved from https://www.brainyquote.com/quotes/nelson_mandela_178789

Matthews, J. K. (2000). *Global odyssey: The autobiography of James K. Matthew*. Nashville, TN: Abingdon Press.

Maxwell, J. C. (2010). *The complete 101 collection: What every leader needs to know*. Nashville, TN: Thomas Nelson.

Mays, B. E., & Nicholson, J. W. (1933). *The Negro's church*. New York, NY: Institute of Social Research.

McClain, W. B. (1984). *Black people in the Methodist Church: Whither thou goest?* Cambridge, MA: Schenkman.

McEllhenney, J. G, Maser, F. E., Rowe, K. E., & Yrigoyan, C. Jr. (1992). *United Methodism in America: A compact history*. Nashville, TN: Abingdon Press.

Medley, B., & Akan, O. (2008). Creating positive change in community organizations: A case for rediscovering Lewin. *Nonprofit Management & Leadership, 18*(4), 485-496. https://doi.org/10.1002/nml.199

Medley, K. (2012). *We as freemen: Plessy v. Ferguson*. New Orleans, LA: Pelican.

Meier, A., & Rudwick, E. (1973). *CORE: A study in the civil rights movement, 1942-1968*. New York, NY. Oxford University Press.

Mennella, H., Strayer, D., & Pravikoff, D. (2016). *Transformational leadership in nursing. Evidence-based care sheet*. Retrieved from https://www.ebscohost.com/assets-sample-content/Transformational_Leadership_in_Nursing.pdf

Methodist Episcopal Church, General Conference. (1936, May 5). *The Daily Christian Advocate*, 88.

Meyer, J. P., Allen, N. J., & Smith, C. H. (1993). Commitment to organizations and occupations: Extension and test of a three-component conceptualization. *Journal of Applied Psychology, 78*(4), 538-551. https://doi.org/10.1037/0021-9010.78.4.538

Mickey Blog. (2018, January 25). *The most inspiring Walt Disney quotes*. Retrieved from https://mickeyblog.com/2018/01/25/ inspiring-walt-disney-quotes/

Miller, S. C. (2015). *Individual readiness for change: The impact of organizational learning culture and learning motivation* (Doctoral dissertation). Available from ProQuest Dissertations and Theses database. (UMI No. 3689197)

Miller, V. D., Johnson, J. R., & Grau, J. G. (1994). Antecedents to willingness to participate in a planned organizational change. *Journal of Applied Communication Research, 22*(1), 5980.

Moore, J. M. (1943a). *The long road to Methodist Union*. Nashville, TN: Abingdon Press.

Moore, J. M. (1943b). *The south today*. New York, NY: Missionary Education Movement of the United States and Canada.

Moorhead, G. I. (2010). *Organizational behavior: Managing people and organizations* (9th ed.). Boston, MA: Cengage Learning.

Morgan, G. (2006). *Images of organization*. Thousand Oaks, CA: SAGE.

Morrison, E.W., & Phelps, C. C. (1999). Taking charge at work: Extra-role efforts to initiate workplace change. *Academy of Management Journal, 42*, 403-419.

Mowday, R. T., Steers, R. M., & Porter, L. W. (1979). The measurement of organizational commitment. *Journal of Vocational Behaviour, 14*, 224-247.

Murray, P. C. (2004). *Methodists and the crucible of race, 1939-1975*. Columbia: University of Missouri Press.

Neuman, G. A., Edwards, J. E., & Raju, N. S. (1994). Organizational development interventions: A meta-analysis of their effects on satisfaction and other attitudes. *Personnel Psychology, 42*, 461-489. doi:10.1111/j.1744-6570.1989.tb00665.x

Nikolaou, I., Gouras, A., Vakola, M., & Bourantas, D. (2007, December). Selecting change agents: Exploring traits and skills in a simulated environment. *Journal of Change Management, 7*(3-4), 291-313. https://doi.org/10.1080/14697010701779173

Northouse, P. G. (2012). *Leadership: Theory and practice* (6th ed.). Thousand Oaks, CA: SAGE.

Norwood, F. A. (1974). *The story of American Methodism*. Nashville, TN: Abingdon Press.

Oliver, R. L. (1974). Expectancy theory predictions of salesmen's performance. *Journal of Marketing Research, 11*, 243-253. Retrieved from https://pdfs.semanticscholar.org/23e3/ f038317c7a63fca5520ce3c5a8e13bd3348e.pdf

Oreg, S. (2003). Resistance to change: Developing an individual differences measure. *Journal of Applied Psychology, 88*(4), 680-692. http://dx.doi.org/10.1037/0021-9010.88.3.680

O'Reilly, A. C. (1989). People and organizational culture: A profile comparison approach to assessing person–organization fit. *The Academy of Management Journal, 34*(3), 487-516.

Organizational change. (2020). In *Cambridge Dictionary Online Dictionary*. Retrieved from https://dictionary.cambridge.org/ dictionary/english/organizational-change

Patton, M. Q. (2002). *Qualitative research & evaluation* (3rd ed.). Thousand Oaks, CA: SAGE.

The People of the United Methodist Church. (n.d.) *Timeline: Methodism in black and white*. Retrieved from https://www.umc.org/en/content/timeline-methodism-in-black-and-white

The People of the United Methodist Church. (2018). *Methodist history: The Uniting Conference of 1968*. Retrieved from https://www.umc.org/en/content/methodist-history-the-uniting-conference-of-1968

Porter, L. W., Steers, R. M., Mowday, R. T., & Boulian, P. V. (1974). Organizational commitment, job satisfaction, and turnover among psychiatric technicians. *Journal of Applied Psychology, 59*(5), 603-609.

Qian, Y. (2007). A communication model of employee cynicism toward organizational change. *Corporate Communications: An International Journal, 13*(3), 319-332. doi:10.1108/13563280810893689

Quarles, B. (1987). *The Negro in the making of America*. New York, NY: Macmillan.

References

Quote analysis: The unexamined life is not worth living. (n.d.). Retrieved from https://schoolworkhelper.net/quote-analysis-the-unexamined-life-is-not-worth-living/

Rahschulte, T. (2007). *Understanding how to change: Inductive determination of how agents of State government plan, lead and sustain change* (Doctoral dissertation). Retrieved from http://digitalcommons.georgefox.edu/gfsb/59

Recardo, R. J. (1995, Spring). Overcoming resistance to change. *Global Business and Organizational Excellence, 14*(2), 5-12. https://doi.org/10.1002/npr.4040140203

Reich, R. B. (1987). Entrepreneurship reconsidered: The team as hero. *Harvard Business Review, 65*(3), 77-83. Retrieved from https://hbr.org/1987/05/entrepreneurship-reconsidered-the-team-as-hero

Reiff, J. T. (2016). *Born of conviction: White Methodists and Mississippi's closed society*. New York, NY: Oxford University

Richey, E. R., Rowe, K. E., & Schmidt, J. (2010). *The Methodist Experience in America: A history* (Vols. 1-2). Nashville, TN: Abingdon Press.

Robbins, S. P., & Coulter, M. (2007). *Management* (9th ed.). London, United Kingdom: Prentice-Hall.

Roberts, A. D. (2017). *Factors that influence successful organizational change in corporations: Examination of change management, employees' reaction to change, and change outcomes* (Doctoral dissertation). Available from ProQuest Dissertations and Theses database. (UMI No. 10746805)

Roosevelt, F. D. (n.d.). *Courage is not the absence of fear but rather the assessment that . . .* Retrieved from https://www.quotespedia.org/authors/f/franklin-d-roosevelt/courage-is-not-the-absence-of-fear-but-rather-the-assessment-that-something-else-is-more-important-than-fear-franklin-d-roosevelt/

Ross, J., & Gray, P. (2006). School leadership and student achievement: The mediating effects of teacher beliefs. *Canadian Journal of Education, 29*(3), 798-822.

Rubin, S. G. (2016). *Brown v. Board of Education: A fight for simple justice.* New York, NY: Holiday House.

Sadler, P. (2001). *Management consultancy: A handbook of best practice.* London, United Kingdom: Kogan Page.

Saka, A. (2002). Internal change agents' view of the management of change problem. *Journal of Organizational Change Management, 16*(5), 480-496.

Santrock, J. W. (2007). *A topical approach to life-span development.* New York, NY: McGraw-Hill.

Sasikala, S., & Anthonyraj, S. V. (2015). Self-efficacy, emotional intelligence and organizational commitment in relation to resistance to change among employees. *Annamalai International Journal of Business Studies & Research, 2015 Special Issue*, 30-35.

Satir, V. (1991). *The Satir model: Family therapy and beyond.* Palo Alto, CA: Science and Behavior Books.

Satterfield, D. W., & Davidson, J. K. (2000). Integrated team approaches to self-management education, care and evaluation. In J. K. Davidson (Ed.), *Clinical diabetes mellitus: A problem oriented approach* (pp. 219-232). New York, NY: Thieme.

Schein, E. H. (1990). Organizational culture. *American Psychologist, 45*(2), 109-119. Retrieved from https://doi.org/ 10.1037/0003-066X.45.2.109

Schein, E. H. (1996). Three cultures of management: *The key to organizational learning. Sloan Management Review, 38(1)*, 9-20. Retrieved from http://citeseerx.ist.psu.edu/viewdoc/ download;jsessionid=29AA1DC8D-6D623615390E08FEDCAA78D?doi=10.1.1.597.3638&rep=rep1&type=pdf

Schilling, H. (1986) *The Reformation and the rise of the early modern state.* Kirkwood, MO: Sixteenth Century Journal.

Schniederjans, D., & Schniederjans, M. (2012). Equity theory based strategies for students on overcoming problems in Ph.D. dissertation committees. *International Journal of Doctoral Studies, 7,* 221-234. https://doi.org/10.28945/1590

Schutte, N. S., Malouff, J. M., & Bhulllar, N. (2009). *The assessing emotions scale.* In J. D. A. Parker, D. H. Saklofske, & C. Stough (Eds.). *Assessing emotional intelligence: Theory, research, and applications* (pp. 119-134). Dordrecht, Netherlands: Springer.

Schwarzer, R., & Jerusalem, M. (1995). *Generalized self-efficacy scale.* In J. Weinman, S. Wright, & M. Johnston (Eds.), *Measures in health psychology: A user's portfolio. Causal and control beliefs* (pp. 35-37). Windsor, United Kingdom: NFER-NELSON.

Seley, M. (2017, October 17). Change is loss and loss requires grief [Blog post]. Retrieved from http://avenuescounselingcenter.org/change-loss-loss-requires-grief/

Semmel, B. (1973). *The Methodist revolution.* New York, NY: Basic Books.

Short, R. H. (1964). *The jurisdictional system.* Nashville, TN: Methodist Publishing House.

Smith, W. T. (1986). *John Wesley and slavery.* Nashville, TN: Abingdon Press.

Stacey, R. D. (1996). The science of complexity: An alternative perspective for strategic change processes. *Strategic Management Journal, 16*(6), 447-485. https://www.jstor.org/ stable/2486790

Sugrue, T. J. (2008). *Sweet land of liberty: The forgotten struggle for civil rights in the North.* New York, NY: Random House.

Sweeney, P. D., & McFarlin, D. B. (2002). *Organizational behavior: Solutions for management.* New York, NY: McGraw-Hill Education.

Tarandach, R. L., & Bartunek, J. M. (2009). A new horizon for organizational change and development scholarship: Connecting planned and emergent change. *Research in Organizational Change and Development, 17*, 1-35. doi:10.1108/S0897-3016(2009)0000017003

Thomas, J. S. (1992). *Methodism's racial dilemma: The story of the central jurisdiction*. Nashville, TN: Abingdon Press.

Tracy, J. D. (1999). *Europe's reformations, 1450-1650*. Lanham, MD: Rowman & Littlefield.

Tran, Q., & Tian, Y. (2013, January 18). Organizational structure: Influencing factors and impact on a firm. *American Journal of Industrial and Business Management, 2013*(3), 229-236. doi:10.4236/ajibm.2013.32028

Tuell, J. M. (2005). *The organization of the United Methodist Church* (2005-2008 ed.). Nashville, TN: Abingdon Press.

United Methodist Church. (2016). *The book of discipline of the United Methodist Church*. Nashville, TN: United Methodist Publishing House.

Van der Voet, J. V., Groeneveld, S., & Kuipers, B. S. (2014). Talking the talk or walking the talk? The leadership of planned and emergent change in a public organization. *Journal of Change Management, 14*(2), 171-191. https://doi.org/10.1080/ 14697017.2013.805160

Ven, A. V., & Sun, K. (2011). Breakdowns in implementing models of organization change. *Academy of Management Perspectives, 25*(3), 58-74. Retrieved from https://doi.org/10.5465/ amp.25.3.zol58

Visagie, C. M., & Steyn, C. (2011). Organisational commitment and responses to planned organisational change: An exploratory study. *Southern African Business Review, 15*(3), 98-121.

Vroom, V. H. (1964). *Work and motivation*. New York, NY: Wiley.

Warren, E. (1954). *Brown v. Board of Education, 347 U.S. 483 (1954)*. Retrieved from https://www.digitalhistory.uh.edu/ disp_textbook.cfm?smtID=3&psid=1120

Warrilow, S. (2012). *Transformational leadership theory—The 4 key components in leading change & managing change*. Retrieved March 15, 2013 from http://EzineArticles.com/? expert=Stephen_Warrilow

Weick, K. F. (2000). Emergent change as a universal in organizations. In M. Beer & N. Nohria (Eds.), *Breaking the code of change* (pp. 223-241). Boston, MA: Harvard Business School.

Welbourne, T. M. (2014). Change management needs a change. *Employment Relations, 41*(4), 17-23. https://doi.org/ 10.1002/ert.21449

Wesley, J. (1958). *The works of Reverend John Wesley* (Vol. 13). Grand Rapids, MI: Zondervan.

White, W. (2001). *Rope and faggot: A biography of Judge Lynch*. Notre Dame, IN: University of Notre Dame.

White, W. W. (2009). The United Methodist Church at 40: How have we done. *Methodist Review, 1*, 57-68. Retrieved from https://methodistreview.org/index.php/mr/article/view/15

Wiener, B. J. (2009, October 19). A theory of organizational readiness for change. *Implementation Science, 4*(67). https://doi.org/10.1186/1748-5908-4-67

Wilstach, F. J. (2010). A dictionary of similes. *Frank J. Wilstach, comp. 1916. A dictionary of similes*. Retrieved from www.bartleby.com/161/

Winstead, P. (1982). *Planned change in institutions of higher learning. In* G. M. Hipps (Ed.), *Effective planned change strategies* (pp. 19-31). San Francisco, CA: Jossey-Bass.

Ye, L. R. (2012). Telecommuting: Implementation for success. *International Journal of Business and Social Science, 3*(15), 20-31. Retrieved from http://www.ijbssnet.com/journals/ Vol_3_No_15_August_2012/4.pdf

Yin, R. K. (2014). *Case study research: Design and methods* (5th ed.). Thousand Oaks, CA: SAGE.

Yukl, G. (2002). *Leadership in organizations* (5th ed.). Englewood Cliffs, NJ: Prentice Hall.

Yukl, G. (2010). *Leadership in organizations* (7th ed.). Upper Saddle River, NJ: Pearson Prentice Hall.